GENERATION X

FIELD GUIDE & LEXICON

GENERATION X

SLACKERS

TWENTYSOMETHINGS

GRUNGE KIDS

13ERS

BUSTERS

THE MOTORBOOTY GENERATION

TWEENERS

LATE BLOOMERS

POST BOOMERS

BOOMLETS

ATARI WAVERS

NINTENDO WAVERS

SKINHEADS

NO FEARS

REPAIR GENERATION

THIRTYSOMETHINGS

MTV GENERATION

ETC.

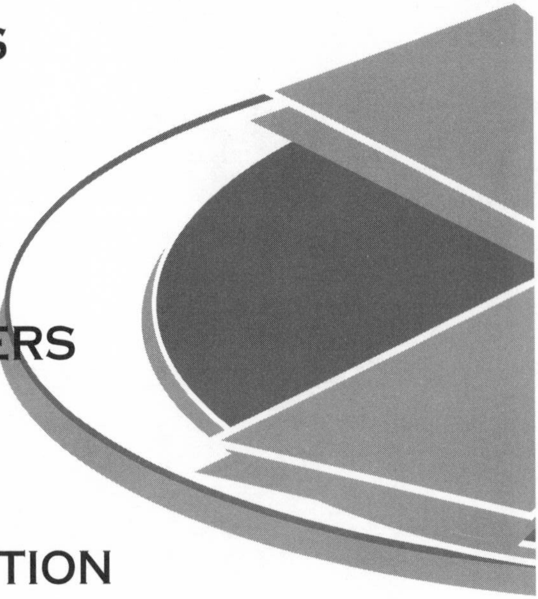

GENERATION X
FIELD GUIDE & LEXICON

by
Vann Wesson

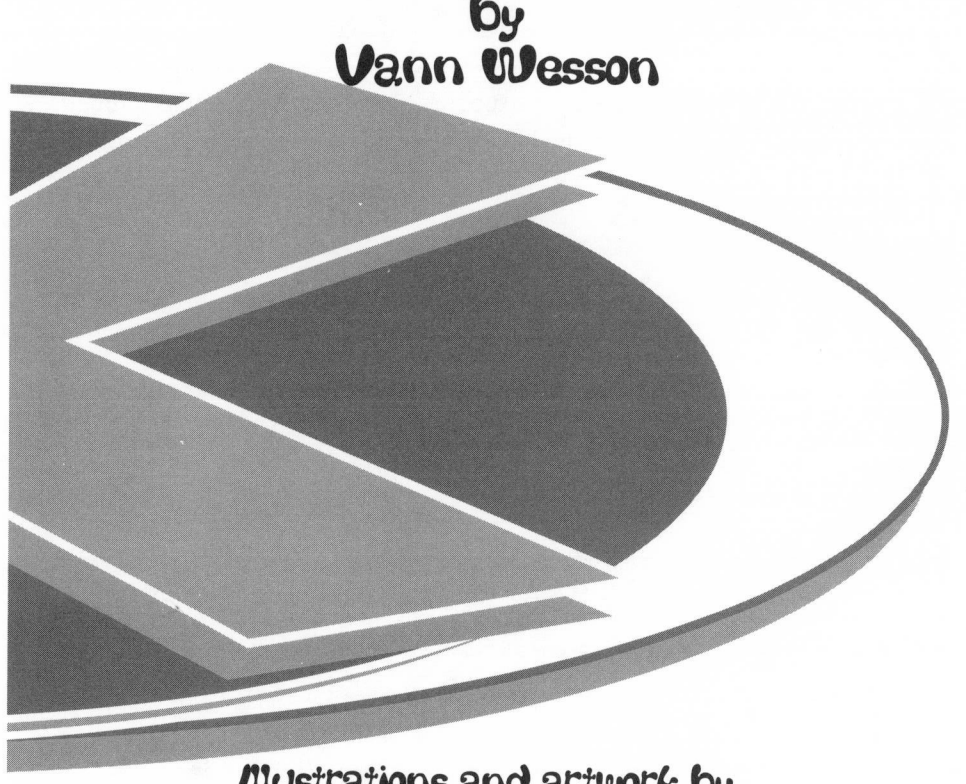

Illustrations and artwork by
Chris Kendall and Erik Aukerman

Research and Editorial Team:

Clea Hantman, former editor Foxy Magazine

Bob (Robert J.) Hawkins, Editor
with the San Diego Union Tribune

Dan P. Whitworth, former managing editor
Axcess Magazine

with Charla Bergman, Erik Bergman, Lance Thayer,
Mathew Casper, Vann Wesson II, Paul Meserole,
and many others

Orion Media

Chris Kendall created the illustrations and cover design. He has created original artwork for clothing, brochures, CD covers, newspapers, and other design applications.

Erik Aukerman designed the Toxic Home Page as well as contributed to the overall book design concept. He has worked in advertising, comic book and trading card illustration, and Web page design.

Both of these excellent artists are in the initial stages of promising careers and are looking for new opportunities for exposure. They can be reached through Orion Media Corporation, the publisher.

Requests for permission to make copies of any part of the work should be mailed to:

Orion Media
3990 Old Town Avenue, Suite 304C
San Diego, California 92110

If you would like to share your comments with us or obtain additional copies. please call us at 1-800-813-3533.

ISBN: 1-887754-05-9

First edition

6 7 8 9 0 1 2 3 4 5 ▪ 9 8 7 6 5 4 3 2 1

Cover design by Chris Kendall

Production by Seaside Publishing Services/Printed in the United States

Publisher Cataloging-in-Publication Data

Wesson, Vann
Generation X field guide and lexicon/written by Vann Wesson; illustrated by Chris Kendall and Erik Aukerman.—1st ed.
p. cm.
LCCN: 96-092165
ISBN: 1-887754-05-9

1. Generation X—United States—Humor. 2. Generation X—United States—Language.
3. Young adults—United States—Humor. 4. Slang—United States—Dictionaries. 5. Marketing I. Title.

HQ799.7.W48 1996   305.23'5'0973

QBI96-20507

SLEEP TIGHT, OLDER AMERICA
GENERATION X IS COMING TO POWER

We are the 79 million or so Americans born from 1961 to 1981—the largest generation America has yet produced.

Like other generations, we represent a wide array of lifestyles and beliefs, but, unlike most previous generations (especially Boomers), we face a diminished economic, ecological, and political environment.

Though many times we are depicted as being too cynical, lazy, and always seeking fun and immediate gratification, we are realistic and serious about our future. We refuse to be placated by the public relations and marketing efforts of Corporate Amerika or to accept the patronizing promises of business-as-usual politicians. We have a strong, healthy skepticism that serves us well.

Hard work is not repulsive to us, but we are unwilling to slave for 40-odd years in an unhappy work environment, just so we can be content in retirement. We want to lead happy, meaningful, and economically secure lives in an unpolluted environment.

We are 79 million strong and we are not afraid of the digital future. Don't forget: We grew up on computers. Atari, Nintendo, and cable TV babysat most of us.

Although it may surprise the Boomer and Silent Generations, who are about to be displaced from power, we will do well and we will do it our way.

DON'T FORGET . . .
YOUR MEDICARE AND SOCIAL SECURITY
DEPEND ON US!

Contents

Generational Chart   front fold-out

Sleep Tight, Older America   v

Introduction   1

LEXICON   even-numbered pages 2–190

TOXIC HOMEPAGES

1. Ethnic Diversity: Look around You   7

2. So What's in a Name? The Generation X Name Tag   13

3. Crash Worship   17

4. Great Millennial Divide: Over 40 Need Not Apply   27

5. What Defines a Generation, Anyway?   37

6. Extreme Sports   53

7. Think Court Lite: New Speedy Justice   57

8. Baby Boomers Offstage   73

9. Raw News/On-Line Awareness   81

10. Spending Their Children's Inheritance   85

11. Millennial Ennui   95

12. Boarding, aka Skateboarding   97

13.	Post-Nuclear Family	129
14.	Raves	141
15.	The Slacker Resume: Personal Spin Control	153
16.	Entrepreneurs	157
17.	Information Overload/Soundbyting	167
18.	Tattoos/Brandings/Scarification	173
19.	Twentysomething/Thirtysomething	175
20.	Advertising/Target X	179
21.	Social (in)Security	185
22.	Hostile Takeover of the United States: Gen X Leveraged Buyout	191
23.	Piercing	192
24.	Environment	194
25.	Employment/Economic Expectations	196
26.	The More Things Change	197
27.	Toxic Homepage Website	199
	Acknowledgments	200

"Oh, great," you're thinking. "Another Generation X book. Another volume of hype that tries to sweep millions of young Americans into a single corner . . . where they won't fit." Well, you're about to be pleasantly surprised. The volume you hold in your hands doesn't presume to speak for an entire generation, nor does it attempt to explain an entire generation or reduce it to a handful of familiar stereotypes. So what is this book, then, if it isn't the latest passenger on the Gen X media bandwagon?

It's about some of our hopes for the future, some of the new ideas we're embracing, and some of the things we can no longer accept as givens. It's a sample, a cross-section of our generation that realizes it can't fit everybody in. It's not a book of rules, or a guide on how to be an "X'er"—but it is a useful volume that may help you understand where we're coming from and where we're going.

It's a fresh, upbeat, humorous, not perfect, but certainly honest (sometimes uncomfortably) insight into the next generation about to take center stage.

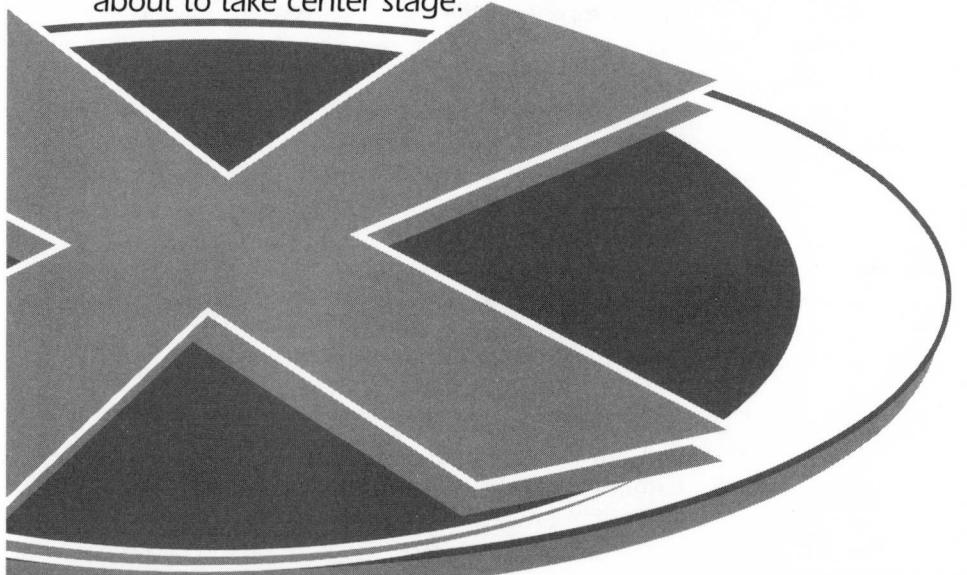

We gathered a team of over twenty-five Gen X'ers to compile the lexicon, create the illustrations, and write the Homepage essays.

Abb

Strange, weird (as in abnormal). "My parents have gone totally abb on me."

Abuzak

Annoying elevator music; a blend of abuse and Muzak.

Acid House

Psychedelic music for the '90s, a cross between '60s psychedelia and disco. According to one source, Acid House was born when British musicians who were into the mid-'80s psychedelic revival visited Chicago and Detroit and then brought **House Music** back to U.K. The result: a heavier, "trippier" form of House Music even more dominated by the Roland 303 and other drum synthesizers.

Acid Jazz

A funky form of music style that merges aspects of jazz, '70s funk, rap, hip-hop, and soul. Legend has it that the name was coined by a British DJ as a joke on the **Acid House** movement of the time. Acid Jazz can be completely sampled (see **Sampling**), it can be played live, but these days it usually combines both. The Greyboy Allstars is one notable group that combines a live band with a DJ. Acid Jazz has its roots in the jazz/funk of the '70s and such Miles Davis albums as 1972's *On the Corner.*

Acid Rock

Loud, distorted, caustic guitar style that ripped through '70s rock like a chain saw.

Action

Fun, exciting, good times; encounters with the opposite sex as usually envisioned by the dorm freshman who has never experienced it. "Looking for some action tonight?"

Action Sports/Extreme Sports

When ordinary exertion is not enough, people push themselves harder. One result: extreme sports, which find young men and women extending the difficulty envelope of outdoor activities like snowboarding and rock climbing, as well as embracing quasi-suicidal sports like bungee jumping. Adrenaline is the key to this danger-enhanced recreational style (see p. 53).

Abuzak

In 1973, the National Stockyards discovered that Muzak calmed cattle and made them easier to slaughter. In the '70s, background music in public became so ubiquitous that the UN passed a resolution confirming individuals' right to silence.

After-Boomers to Alternative

After-Boomers

Those born after the post-World War II baby boom—from about 1965–1975 (see also **Baby Busters** and **Post-Boomers**). This is a group united mainly by its disdain for such labels.

Aggro

1) Intense action in any sport where the action pumps up the adrenaline. When Andre Agassi plays tennis, he's all aggro all the time.

2) Mad; extremely angry. "My mother went aggro on me when she saw my purple hair."

Alley Scoring

Dumpster diving/dining; "diving for dinner," eating out of the dumpster. You can also apply the term to the time-honored practice of recycling furniture and other cool stuff left out for the trash collector.

Alpha Geek

The most knowledgeable, technically proficient person in the office or work group. Befriend the alpha geek: Bring gifts of **Jolt Cola,** Ding-Dongs and Cheez-Wiz. Some day this person will save your career. "Ask Larry, he's the alpha geek around here."

Alterna Rock/Alternative Rock

A term rendered nearly meaningless after it was co-opted as a media catch-phrase for rock deemed too raw or underproduced to fit into popular radio formats. Once **alternative** became a sign of credibility, as blue jeans were in the '60s, record company marketing forces jumped on the term and labeled most folk–punk–acoustic guitar acts with a grunge look as "alternative." Multimillion-dollar corporations actually stamp out crude press releases on rough recycled paper for bands they wish to signify as "alternative."

Alternachick/Alternachic

Today's alternative woman, identified by her second-hand store clothes—flannels, baggy jeans, T-shirts—and complete disdain for anything "commercial" or mass market.

Alternative

A non-conforming lifestyle that expresses disdain for anything mainstream. For a generation that lacks an identity, disdaining labels and all things commercial has become an identity in itself. As it was with hippies, there is a mix of idealists, opportunists, and wannabes. Even Ralph Lauren pushes a line of clothing that exploits the alternative look.

Alternachick

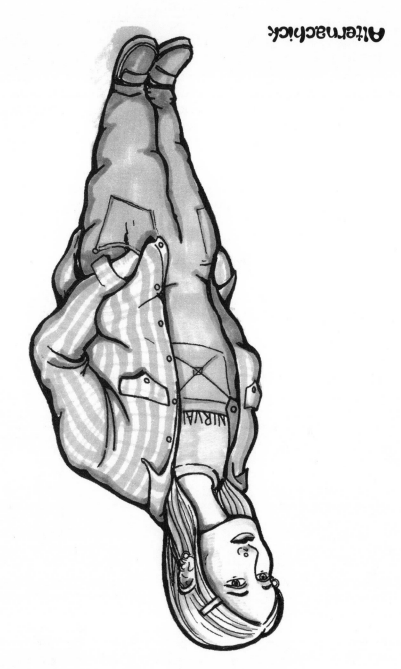

TOXIC HOME PAGE

Alternative Folkie

Refers to a guitar player, acoustic or electric, who is often hippie in nature and adores the Grateful Dead but usually sings deeply pessimistic odes to abuse, dysfunction, black holes, a hopeless future, date rape, dissolution, death, and anything commercial.

Ambient

Spacy, atmospheric music, more preoccupied with aural coloration and textural layering than a drumbeat. Often used in a dance club's "chill-out" room, courtesy of the techno-shaman with his fingers on the DJ turntables.

Ambient-Dub

Ambient with a danceable beat added, often overlayered with "dub" production effects (echoes, rewinds) derived from reggae.

Ambrosia

Any delicious drink. Literally, "the nectar of the gods."

Amerika

The land of disenchantment. Also, AmeriKKKa—the land of disenchantment from the perspective of minorities.

Amped Up

To be extremely excited. "I am so totally amped up over tomorrow's Hootie and the Blowfish concert."

Anal

Obsessive; often viewed as uncool. Sometimes used to describe an older generation's habit of delaying pleasure and enjoyment and condemning as "slackers" anyone who wants to enjoy life before reaching age 65. **Alpha geeks** can be anal about their work, especially if they spend their waking lives writing code in software sweatshops.

Angst

1) A feeling of great anxiety, worry, restlessness, and depression—frequently without any identifiable cause. For **Generation X,** angst has taken widespread use both in print and in conversation to describe feelings and situations of both great and small magnitude. In this sense, it is considered a psychological problem.

2) Angst also has philosophical associations that indicate deeper meaning and problems; translated as dread, a pensiveness over a

(continued)

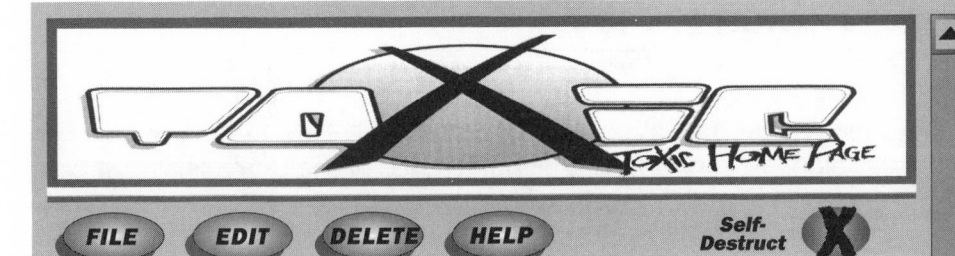

ETHNIC DIVERSITY: LOOK AROUND YOU

X'ers are the most ethnically diverse generation in U.S. history. Between immigration trends and changing national birthrate characteristics, we are much more "ethnic" than the general population. How much more ethnic are we? Thirty-three percent more Asian, 26 percent more Hispanic, 17 percent more African American. And Y Generation is even more ethnic.

Fear of these changing population patterns may help explain why Congress is starting to yank the immigration welcome mat from the U.S. front porch there in New York Harbor.

(continued on p. 9)

situation. Samuel Beckett, Jean-Paul Sartre and Franz Kafka explored angst in their plays and fiction. For these writers, the self is alone in confronting the indifference of the universe. Angst also helps to fill coffeehouses with pensive young men in goatees, writing poetry as they nurse a cup of Sumatran blend.

Angst-ridden

The state of being wherein one is riddled with anxiety and depression because of a surrounding doom due to the tension and stress of a consumption-oriented society. The tool used by business today to keep employee costs at a minimum. "Everyone I know is angst-ridden from trying to survive in Corporate America on a **McSalary**." (See **McSalary**: see also **McJob**.)

Anti-manifesto

A declaration of what is not believed, contrary to a manifesto or public declaration of a set of beliefs. One of the more powerful came in John Lennon's song "God," in which he professed in litany form: "I don't believe in magic/I don't believe in I Ching/I don't believe in Bible/I don't believe in tarot . . ." and so on through Kennedy, Buddha, Zimmerman (Bob Dylan's real name), and the Beatles.

AOL

America Online, currently the largest commercial online service in the world. CompuServe and Prodigy round out the Big Three. Smaller commercial services include Delphi. Two giants, AT&T and Microsoft, have also recently jumped into the online competitive fray.

Aqua Boot

To vomit in the water.

Argot

A jargon or speech used by those in the same line of work, or who share the same way of life, in order to conceal the true importance of what is said—as in the jargon of tramps, criminals, beatniks, hippies, psychologists, etc. Every generation creates its own argot as it attempts to define itself.

As If

Expression of doubt: "I think you should try dating John. He's ugly but sweet." Response: "As if!"

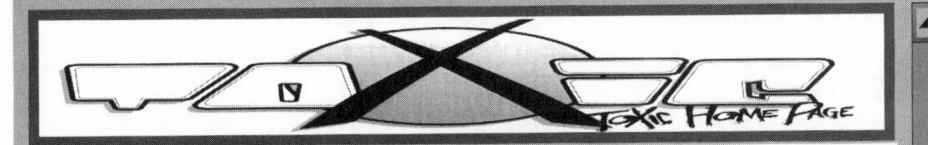

ETHNIC DIVERSITY *(continued from p. 7)*

Luckily, there is an opposite trend as well. TV programming and motion pictures have finally begun to portray Asians, Hispanics, and African Americans in mainstream roles of power and respect, instead of as only running groceries and laundries, as gardeners, car washers and tequila-drinking desperadoes, or as servants, maids, and sleazy, drug-addicted musicians. To name a few: **Rosie Perez** in her leading female roles in numerous movies, **Russell Wong** of the TV series *Vanishing Son* and star **Denzel Washington,** who, after saving democracy in *The Pelican Brief* and averting nuclear holocaust in *Crimson Tide* certainly deserves our respect.

Take a look at the ads in magazines, newspapers, on TV, and billboards. You will probably see "The United Colors of Benetton." Maybe our country is finally learning to respectfully acknowledge all of its members—or maybe Corporate America has just discovered new target markets and is busy drawing bull's-eyes on previously "unseen" minority groups. Conscience or capitalism? It doesn't matter—the results are the same. As minorities, we have tremendous influence on the language, role model selection, music, and tastes of our generation and society. Ethnic acceptance may still have a hard road ahead of it, but we're on our way.

ANGST-RIDDEN

A friend said that everyone of our generation is "angst-ridden." Maybe we have something in common with Winnie, Samuel Beckett's character in *Happy Days*. Winnie is buried to her waist in sand in Act One. In Act Two she is buried to her neck. She attempts to keep the demons of existential angst away by maintaining a constant prattle and distracting herself through well-timed but meaningless activity with objects in her shopping bag, and, perhaps, a daily song, if sung at the right time, neither too early nor too late. Her greatest fear is that she won't be able to fill the time between the bell that wakes her and the bell that says it's time to sleep.

Atari Wavers

Anyone born in the late 1960s.

Auteur

Originally used to describe a movie director who exercises total creative control and exhibits a strong personal style. The rising number of small independent computer software and multimedia design shops are breeding a new type of digital auteur who finds unfettered expression in creative CD-ROM content, design, and interfaces.

Auteurs sans Direction

Directors without direction. The many low-budget film jockeys who try to follow Quentin Tarrantino's non-linear style in *Pulp Fiction* may end up as auteurs sans direction.

Autodidact's Journey

A journey of self-learning.

Babe Magnet

An object, technique, or person that women supposedly find irresistible. Popular babe magnets include a nice car, stylish clothes, attractive looks, and (the old standby) a fistful of cash.

Babefest

A party at which there are many girls, the ultimate party of the imagination. "There were forty babes and me" *(Wayne's World)*.

Baboos

Baby Boomers.

Baby Batter

Sperm.

Baby Boomers

Those 78 million Americans born between 1943 and 1960. This generation was noted for "questioning and challenging the establishment," but now they are the establishment and vigorously defend the status quo. Boomers are the ones who decided that **Generation X** should be the next target of big business and its advertising minions. They might mistrust us and mock us, but they'll be happy to separate us from our money (see page 73).

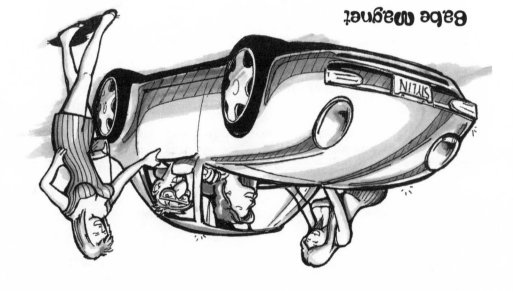

Babe Magnet

Baby Busters

The portion of **Generation X** born between 1960 and 1975, when birthrates dropped dramatically, ending the **Baby Boomer** bulge.

Baby Pop

A young man.

Bag

To harass or continually criticize. "If you don't stop bagging on me, I'm leaving!"

Bail

To leave. "Some babe magnet this party turned out to be. Let's bail."

Baked

Stoned, usually on marijuana. A milder, gentler high. Less corrosive than the brain-frying harder drugs that gave rise to "See the fried egg. This is your brain. This is your brain on drugs."

Baldwin

An attractive guy; male version of a **Betty.**

Ballistic

1) To go crazy; to lose control of emotions. "Her dad went ballistic when he saw her nose ring and shoulder tattoo."

2) Armed gang warfare. "Let's get ballistic!" (from *New Jack City*).

3) Going full out on anything.

Banana Hammock

Bikini briefs that old men sport at the beach. (See **Grape Smuggler**.)

Banda Music

Rowdy Mexican brass bands that carry the oompah of polka-rooted music to new heights of exuberance.

Bandwidth

What we all need to drive faster on the Information Superhighway. The greater the bandwidth, the faster data can be transmitted. Think of a two-lane road versus a five-lane highway.

Bank

1) To earn good money at a job or commercial venture. As in "He's making bank in the software-design business."

(continued)

SO WHAT'S IN A NAME?:
ORIGIN OF GENERATION X NAME TAG

GENERATION X: A 1960s English paperback about sex, drugs, and rock'n'roll in the London mod scene.

GENERATION X: The 1970–1980s British band led by Billy Idol and Tony James, created from the breakup of their previous band, Chelsea. The name was taken from the paperback novel (see above). Generation X broke up in the early '80s. Billy Idol went on to a successful solo career with songs like "Your Generation," "Dancing with Myself," "White Wedding," "Eyes without a Face" and "Flesh for Fantasy." Many people no longer take Billy Idol very seriously.

GENERATION X: The 1991 novel by Douglas Coupland, subtitled *Tales for an Accelerated Culture*, that depicts the lives of young Americans with few options beyond "low-pay, low-prestige, low-dignity, no-future McJobs." When asked how he thought up the name for this generation, Coupland replied, "I didn't come up with the name for a generation. I just came up with a title for a novel." Even so, Coupland was pretty much on target in this book, especially in his perception of Generation X as one that resists being pigeon-holed by demographics and targeted by advertisers.

GENERATION X: 1990s target-market term that alerted the media and advertisers that there was a vast portion of the American populace that they were ignoring. Karen Ritchie, in her book *Marketing to Generation X,* examined the possibilities of targeting this generation as an untapped consumer group in extensive detail. (Ms. Ritchie herself is a Boomer.) Media and advertising now try their darndest to keep up with what's going on with this generation, although sometimes the best they can do is fill their commercials with actors in flannel shirts and have them drink lots of coffee.

GENERATION X: A handy term that cannot begin to describe the true diversity of a generation that is, still, resistant to being manipulated by media, advertising, and politicians. "Generation X" isn't about to sit still and let anyone on TV tell them who they are, what they think, or what they should buy. Even so, it seems likely that this is the term history books will use to describe those of us born between 1961 and 1981.

2) An action or event that is guaranteed or promised. As in "You can bank on it."

3) Money in one's pocket; **fundage.**

Bank Geek

The new generation of post-high school nerds. A bank geek is usually conservative, quiet, and prissy (inwardly harboring, of course, tattoo fantasies).

Barfogenesis

Seasick feeling some people get using virtual-reality headsets, caused by the eyes registering movements that the inner ears don't.

Barney

Moron; jerk. From that putridly plush purple pediatric pilgrim plying the planet via morning Plexiglas programming. When you hear "What a Barney!"—consider yourself insulted.

Basing

From the term *debase.* If done correctly, basing is a cruel and accurate appraisal of one's contemporaries grounded in honesty and transmitted through sarcasm. If done ineptly, it can be grounds for slander.

Base

To argue.

Basse Couture

"Low culture"; the opposite of *haute couture* ("high culture").

Bathetic

Worse than pathetic.

Bazillion

A bazillion is used to describe extreme quantities of anything—like how many ducats the average Gen X'er would like to have (see **Ducats/Ducketts**).

B-Boy/B-Girl

One who is wise to the street criteria put forth in hip-hop music and lifestyle. Also a rap music devotee. The B stands for "beat," which is crucial to the music. Thanks to white rappers The Beastie Boys, this can now apply across racial divisions.

Barfogenesis

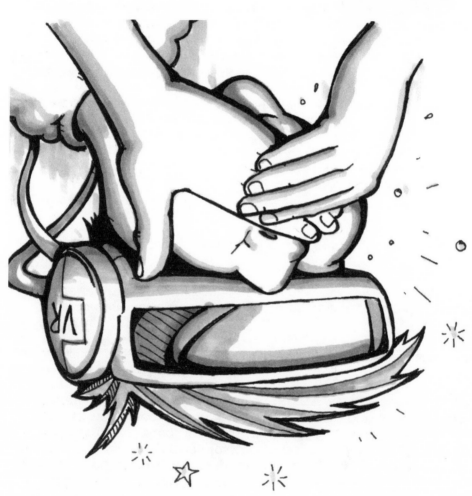

B-Boy Stance

Defiant pose typically struck by crossing arms across the chest and standing square on an opponent. The term is common to rap and hip-hop music culture.

BBS

Bulletin Board System. Computer systems accessed by a modem; often free areas devoted to specific interest groups in which you can post messages or respond to others. As the World Wide Web grows more commercialized, it is possible that BBS sites will return to the popularity they enjoyed in the pioneering days of online communication.

Beam Me Up Scotty

Smoking crack.

Beast, the

Hip-hop slang for anything that is out of control. "The new Cypress Hill record is the beast, man!"

Beat Boy

Rapper, singer, poet; vocal artist who uses the rap format of expression.

Beavis and Butthead

Two **MTV** cartoon characters, Beavis and Butthead do short skits and talk-overs while bands perform on videos. Beavis and Butthead project every puerile behavior dreaded and despised by parents. They have attitude. They are sugar junkies who hate school and parents. They are preoccupied with sexual innuendo. They are blissfully ignorant. Is it any wonder they are popular?

Beckettian Consciousness

Samuel Beckett, playwright and novelist of the mid-twentieth century, is identified with what is called the "theater of the absurd." His most famous play is *Waiting for Godot*, in which the characters simply wait for a mysterious character who never appears. They seem to know little about Godot and can't quite remember why they are waiting. The characters embody the meaninglessness and emptiness of modern Western society. The stage is barren, except for a leafless tree. There is no reconciliation, no redemption, no hope; it is a work of uncompromising estrangement. Time stretches out before the characters as empty space filled with meaningless chatter and

(continued)

CRASH WORSHIP

While there have always been select groups of people who operate outside the realm of "normal" society, this generation's unique boundary-slashing ideals coupled with the penchant for back-to-nature extremes, has produced several fringe groups that defy any kind of categorization and baffle those who come into contact with the oft-unkept band of merry freaks.

One such faction is Crash Worship.

Crash Worship are Southern California's answer to "A Quest for Fire." Imagine, if you will, an exact reenactment of said movie, with guitars. A Crash Worship show is not rock'n'roll. Don't go there expecting assigned seating, beer vendors, and the like. Expect everything else. They are a troupe, not a band. Their membership is flexible and their music is merely an excuse. An excuse for what? Getting primitive.

On one hand, their show is debauchery incarnate. Fire, alcohol, painted bodies, nudity, sometimes sex. One show in New Orleans went out into the streets during Mardi Gras and resulted in cars getting turned over, fires, etc.—all to a good beat. The revealers revealed with no compunction for anything else. The police were called and some of the troupe ended up in the pokey. It is doubtful that anyone in attendance would have traded it for anything.

The way society perceives these people is as bohemian degenerates, with no respect for society at all. But this is a typically bigoted assumption. They are outside of society, there's no doubt about that. But they put themselves there solely by being free. As free as they are able to be. Their shows seem to be based on instinct and following that instinct, whether it be musical or physical. They are performance artists and their art knows no borders, internal or external. In this modern era of strict and structured living, they are reminding people that they don't have to be drones, that they can experience themselves a little deeper if they desire.

Crash Worship may be a relatively new group, but what they do is older than history. What they do is spiritual.

partially remembered experiences that have lost all value. The characters are lost and uncomprehending—a dismal state of consciousness that many of us know all too well (see p. 95).

Beef
A butt fall from a skateboard.

Benched
To be reprimanded.

Betty
A hot girl; pretty woman or girl.

Bhangra Music
A hybrid of North Indian music (particularly Punjabi drumming and long, sinuous vocal lines) with contemporary Western rhythms and strategies, from **house music** to reggae to rapping. A long shot for mainstream acceptance, but one that reaches South Asian fans in England and the United States.

Biddies
Baby Boomers in Debt.

Biff
Fail; trip; mess up.

Biffed
When a surfer gets thrown out by a wave.

Big Day Out
A two-week music carnival and festival in Australia. It has been described as Australia's answer to **Lollapalooza**.

Bigtime
Totally; very. "He lost it bigtime."

Bills
Cash money, ducats, bank, moolah. Essential for those pricey microbrews favored by Gen X'ers. Those without bills have spare change. Maybe enough to brown bag it with a malt liquor.

Betty

Binary Star Configuration/Bi-Star

Any grouping of two things that seem inseparable, for whatever reason. "Pierced nipples and crotch tattoos are totally bi-star." A Porsche and a balding Boomer are bi-star.

Bio-Break

Euphemism employed by avid computer hacks for using the toilet.

Biohazard

1) Unhealthy-looking, smelly person.

2) Anything dangerous to the environment.

3) The name of a metal-rap band from New York.

Biscuit

Easy.

Biscuithead

Lame person; a dork.

Bit Spit

Any form of digital correspondence.

Bit Stream

1) Transmission of binary signals through a computer chip.

2) The excited flow of information from one person to another. "She was bit streaming ideas at me so fast that I couldn't grasp half of what she was saying!"

Bitch Basket

Volkswagen Cabriolet—a favorite among sorority girls and airheads. Rarely parallel parked.

Bitnik

A person who uses coin-operated computers at cyber-trendy coffeehouses.

Bitraking

Journalistic practice of trolling the **Internet** in search of stories.

Bizotic

BIZarre plus exOTIC equals weird.

Bitch Basket

Blase

More than indifferent; don't know, don't care. It's "We don't care that we don't know."

Blather

Nonsensical, self-serving conversation—but blather is in the eye of the beholder.

Blendo

A music-video style combining different media from different sources: type, computer graphics, animation, video, audio, etc. Similar to multimedia, but more often used to describe a collage effect. Also called meltomedia.

Blip-mitment

Stunted relationship characterized by shallow talk, malt liquor, and infrequent (but safe) sex. Shorter and less involved than a commitment.

Blow Chow/ Blow Chunks

To vomit.

Blow Off

To jilt a partner; to skip out on a commitment or meeting. "She blew him off for that nerd."

Blue Steeler

A particularly virile erection. "She saw the blue steeler. I heard a barely audible sigh, her lips quivered and parted slightly. She knew what I had in mind."

Blunt

See **Phillies Blunt.**

Boarder

Skateboarder. Two types: a) Verts (verticals) use skate ramps and specially configured bowls; and b) Street Skaters ply roadways and sidewalks. There are often bad vibes between the two groups. Boarder can also apply to snowboarders and boogieboarders (See **Action Sports/Extreme Sports** and p. 97).

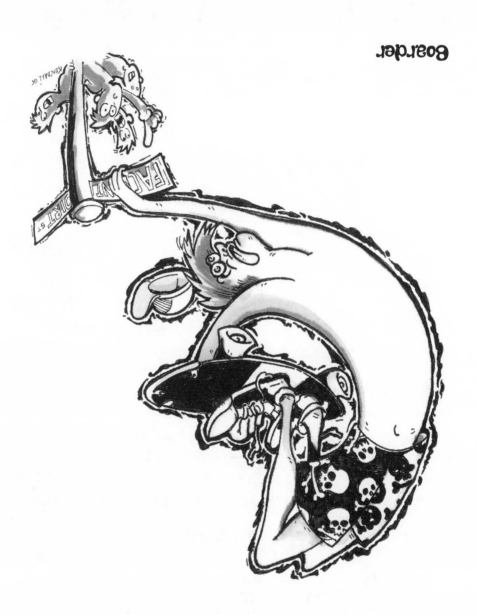

Boarder

Body Surfing

Part of moshing (see **Mosh Pit**) where a person is lifted above the crowd and passed around at a concert. This is group participation, a team sport, so everyone plays, although it's not unusual for everyone to become distracted and drop the surfer.

Boff

To have sexual intercourse. Boff would imply a shoddy job on a complete stranger. You would not boff your boyfriend/girlfriend or husband/wife unless your relationship was soon to be past history.

Bogart

To hoard, as in "Don't bogart that joint." The meaning has remained unchanged since the early sixties.

Bogosity

Rudeness. "Can you believe the bogosity of that dweeb?" Derived from original negative meaning of **bogus.**

Bogue

Smoke a cigarette.

Bogulate

To surf badly.

Bogus

Totally cool. "What a bogus car!" The meaning has come 180 degrees from its original, which meant something was fake and bad.

BOHICA

Bend Over Here It Comes Again. The expression rises out of the resignation that results from a feeling of powerlessness, an inability to determine one's fate.

Boho Enclave

A place or area where the inhabitants live an alternative bohemian lifestyle. For example, the boho enclave of Athens, Georgia, where R.E.M. was discovered in the early '80s.

Boink

To have sex.

Boinkfest

To have sex in quantity.

Body Surfing

BOOMERANGS

Most often the return is for economic reasons; to reasonably survive the "Harsh Realm" of X'er employment economics. Many end up with a reasonable disposable income that is disposed of on music, music and computer equipment, clothing, and cars . . . enjoyment.

"Of course, life back home with the folx is unsatisfying . . . if it wasn't, people would live with their parents forever."

Bolivian Marching Powder

Cocaine. Derived from the famous opening line of novelist Jay McInerny's *Bright Lights, Big City*.

Bomb/The Bomb

The best/to be the best.

Boo

Stupid.

Boo Ya

Thank you very much. (Sarcastically, as in "No applause, I know I'm great.")

Boogerhead

An affectionate nickname for a friend.

Book

To leave quickly. "Let's book outta this dump." Another resurrected term.

Boomerangs

Those X'ers who return to the Boomer parent family nest after flying around on their own for a while (see page 25).

Boomlets

Kids of Baby Boomers.

Boost/Boosting

To steal/stealing. "Some **Barney** boosted my backpack."

Bound-and-Hagged

Staying home on Friday or Saturday night with your boyfriend/girlfriend. Entered the language by way of the *New York Times* "Grunge Hoax" (see **Grunge Hoax**).

Box

Stereo, boom box, or any equipment that provides music.

Brad's Mom

A technophobic customer, from the language spoken at Microsoft headquarters (as in Lillian Silverberg, mother of a Microsoft executive). It is the most common standard of applicability and clarity. Software developers half-jokingly say "Can Brad's mom figure this out?"

GREAT MILLENNIAL DIVIDE:
OVER 40 NEED NOT APPLY

We stand with the future on the north rim of the Great Millennial Divide. Across that impassable Grand Canyon stumble the generations that came before us, languishing in the past they created. The Boomer and older generations belong to the last century of the Second Millennium. We belong to the Twenty-First Century, and we're going to kick the Third Millennium off right.

Aging the Generations by Oldest Members

In Year	Y Generation those born in 1982 will be	Generation X those born in 1961 will be	Boomers those born in 1943 will be	Silents those born in 1925 will be
1997	16	37	55	73
2000	19	40	58	76
Great Millennium Divide				
2004	23	44	62	80
2008	27	48	66	
2012	31	52	70	
2016	35	56	74	
2020	39	60	78	
2024	43	64	82	
2028	47	68		

By 2004, we will probably be in the White House. After all, Kennedy was only 43 when he took office, and Clinton was only 44. Why shouldn't we elect our own generation to represent us instead of the old-guard, business-as-usual crowd? They put this country into a mess only to leave it for us to straighten it out—so we will. But we won't do it their way.

(continued on p. 29)

Brady/Brady Bunch

The TV family many X'ers grew up watching. A widow with three girls married a widower with three sons. Living together in a bright, cheery house, they became the new nuclear family. An unreal alternative to reality.

Brah

Surfer version of bro (see **Bro**).

Brainiac

A smart person. "Let those brainiacs figure it out."

Brazilification

1) The process by which the First World indebts the Third World and sends it on a downward economic and social spiral. The consequence of this downward spiral is a two-tiered country consisting of the very rich and the impoverished masses.

2) The widening gulf between the rich and the poor, accompanied by the disappearance of the middle classes.

Break Out

To leave.

Brechtian Objectivity

From the Marxist playwright and literary theorist Berthold Brecht. In his theoretical writings, he was interested in the relation of art (its capacity to undermine forces of oppression and domination) to politics. In particular, how art can transform the false consciousness of bourgeois society. The emphasis of art and visual form over readability in many contemporary GenX **zines** (see **Zines**) can sometimes be viewed in a similar light.

Breeder

Homosexual term for a heterosexual.

Brewsky/Brewski

A beer.

Brick

To be scared, as in "We saw their guard dog and bricked." Probably from the expression "to shit a brick" as an indication of fear.

(continued from p. 27)

The old-guard politicians represent their peers, that huge federal-debt-producing, paycheck-robbing, Medicare/Social Security crowd. We won't fall for their empty rhetoric any more. They don't share our concerns. They barely know us. They don't even know how to speak to us. But that doesn't really matter, does it?

You see, with the passing of every two-year interval between national elections, 8 million of us join the nation's electorate, while 6 million Silent Generation voters disappear. By 1998, our generation will be the largest American group of voting-age adults—larger than the Boomers, and twice as large as the surviving "Silents."

What was that cliché the Boomers were so fond of chanting as they shook their fists at the establishment? "Power to the people." They are the establishment now . . . we are the people.

The time is long overdue to set right the mistakes of the past . . . and we're the generation to do it.

Bro
Dude talk for brother or friend.

Broke
1)"To be ugly. From "So ugly the mirror broke."

2)To end. "The mosh pit scene broke, man, so we booked."

Bucked
To get naked. From "buck naked."

Budded Out
Stoned on pot.

Buds
Marijuana.

Budster
A combination of buddy and buster. (May also be spun off the term *dudester*.) Popularized in a *Saturday Night Live* sketch.

 Buff

Describes a well-muscled body. It probably evolved from "buffing one's car," implying that buff is only as real as the surface of things. It may also come from "in the buff," as in naked (see **Exerhead**).

Buffed Out
In a primo state of **buff.**

Buggin'
1) When you think someone is lying.

2) To be irritated or perturbed; flipping out.

Bump'n
(Pronounced bum-pun). Of the highest quality, as in clothes or music. Sometimes extended to "bump'n like a mug" for emphasis.

Bun Floss
An extremely small G-string bikini that rides up between the buttocks and displays the cheeks like wrapped meat products found in the deli case at a supermarket.

Buff/Exerhead

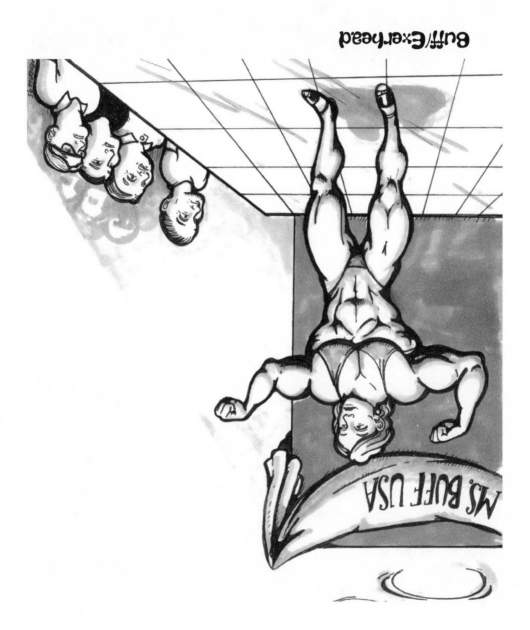

MS. BUFF USA

Buppies

1) British Urban Professionals.

2) Black Urban Professionals.

Burb

Suburb.

Burn-outs

High school big-wigs who later end up working as security guards at liquor stores in seedy parts of town.

Burner

Someone who smokes a lot of marijuana.

Bust a Cap

To shoot a bullet from a gun. Refers to a bullet as a "cap" or to the practice aimed at wounding a competing gang member in the kneecap.

Bust a Few

To surf. "Lets go bust a few while the **sets** (see **Set**) are hot."

Bust a Move

1) To dance. Showing your best stuff on the dance floor.

2) Making a move on a **freak.**

3) To get going; to leave.

Bust a Rhyme

To rap.

Buster

Jerk, a **Barney.**

Butt

1) Extremely ugly.

2) Undesirable.

Butter

Girls.

Buttnuggett

Cool.

Burn-outs

Buy Doody

Juvenile code for buying marijuana. Cryptic enough to mean anything, yet specific enough by the knowing glance. Since so many Generation X'ers still live at home, parents who overhear the term can be told it refers to clothes, food, CDs, etc., thereby allaying parental concerns.

Buzz

1) A good word, usually about a particular band. "I've heard a good buzz on Archers of Loaf."

2) Stoned. As in "to cop a buzz."

3) A gauge for consumption of alcohol, pot, and other low-grade drugs. A buzz is the beginning of getting loaded.

Buzz Bin

MTV's name for the heavy rotation of selected alternative or cutting edge video clips. Getting placed in the Bin will generally insure gold or platinum sales status. For connoisseurs of small club bands, this honor ruins their cool favorites by exposing them to the mass audience. Just look at what MTV's Buzz Bin spin did for Green Day. They went from **indie** punkers to corporate cash cows (see p. 91).

Caffiend

Java head; caffeine fiend.

Cakes

Women or girls.

Cameo

A type of haircut popular among young black males; the hair is trimmed short on the sides and flat or angular on top. White version is known as a **mullet.**

Cash Harvesting

Would usually occur on a Friday, when the slacker receives his hourly **McWages** (see **McSalary**). Harvesting implies a surplus and even celebration, which is ironic. Isn't it?

Cashed

Used up, finished. As in someone who has cashed in her chips.

Catch One

Getting a buzz (see **Buzz**) or rush on drugs or alcohol.

Caffeine addiction: That stuff be calling' me, callin' me, man, and I gotta go to it. (*New Jack City*)

Caffiend

Man with a gun in a coffee shop: "Just give me the coffee and nobody gets hurt."

Cellular Autonomy
The freedom to roam, communicate, stay connected, and even operate a business from anywhere via cellular phone.

Checking
Pulling down another's swimsuit shorts from behind as a surprise.

Cheeba/Chiba
Originally a Spanish-language term for heroin; outside Hispanic neighborhoods it has come to mean dope in general. Some now use it to refer to marijuana, particularly a descendant of the "skunk" breed of the plant.

Cheeky Mama
A sassy chick; chauvinistic term for an assertive woman.

Cheesedog
1) A friend who has erred or done something uncharacteristically nerdy. Used to shake them back into sensibility.
2) A generic loser of the male kind with delusions of grandeur. They see themselves as "topdog" but the rest of the world sees a "cheesedog."

Cheesemuffin
Female equivalent of a **cheesedog.**

Chekhovian Instinct
When two people talk right past each other, from the play *The Cherry Orchard* by Russian playwright Chekhov. It is sometimes used to describe the inability of status quo politicians and much of Corporate Amerika to see or communicate with **post-Boomer** generations.

Chill Out
Calm down; hang out; relax.

Chillin'
Hanging out.

Chiphead
Computer enthusiast.

Chips and Salsa
Slang for computer hardware (chips) and related software (salsa).

WHAT DEFINES A GENERATION, ANYWAY?

The real puzzle in getting through to the end of the twentieth century (and beyond) is figuring out where all these generational labels came from—and what they really mean. Obviously, people born fifty years ago had a different upbringing than people born twenty years ago, along with different values and different expectations. They all did things that later generations would (Or will) think are ridiculous, too. Human nature doesn't change that much, but here we are harping about Generation This and That. Who thought this stuff up, anyway?

Part of the confusion lies with historians and sociologists, who need handy labels to stick on groups of people so their dissertations will sound impressive. But not everyone agrees on the point where one generation leaves off and another begins. According to one definition (Landon Y. Jones, *Great Expectations*, 1980), the Baby Boomer Generation began in 1946 and ended in 1964. The name comes from a very real upsurge in births right after World War II—but is it realistic to lump eighteen years' worth of babies into the same group? Someone born the year after Hiroshima exploded didn't grow up in the same world as a kid born the year after Kennedy died. William Strauss and Neil Howe (*Generations,* 1991) moved the start of the Boomer Generation to 1943, before the war ended—and before the actual population boom. So how good are these labels?

Strauss and Howe were thinking along these lines when they developed the Cohort Group Theory, a more flexible definition of generations (which we go along with). To clarify matters, they split the definition of a generation into two

(continued on p. 41)

Choiceamundo
Fantastic.

Chops
Very impressive technique, often musical. Originally referred to skill with instruments played by the mouth; now used to describe virtuosity on any instrument, or technical skill in any art form: "The Diz had monster chops" or "Dig his programming chops."

Chronic
1) An extremely potent variety of marijuana.

2) The title of a rap album by Dr. Dre.

Chuppie
Chicano Urban Professional.

Circling the Drain
Though originally medical slang for a patient near death who refuses to give up the ghost, it is now also used to describe projects that have no more life in them but refuse to die. "That coffee shop is finally closing. It's been circling the drain for the last six months."

Clean Peeler
Perfectly formed wave (in the eyes of a surfer).

Clock
1) To watch. "Clock that **Clydesdale**." (See **Clydesdale**.)

2) To kill. "I'm going to clock that **dude**."

Club Kids' Style
Flamboyant, almost absurd wardrobes, often balanced atop massive platform shoes: this is the look of the club kid. Flowing from an original scene in New York, the look became *de rigeur* for a certain element of the **rave** scene. Passing out of style, it still has its diehard proponents and continues to pop up as "new" in the Midwest, Las Vegas, and everywhere else raves are becoming popular for the first time.

Club Music
Post-disco electronic rhythms that propel club-goers into the wee hours. A proliferation of sub-genres comes and goes, calibrated in beats per minute, including techno, jungle, house, rave, dub, tribal, and ambient. All club genres fall under the record-company category

(continued)

Circling the Drain

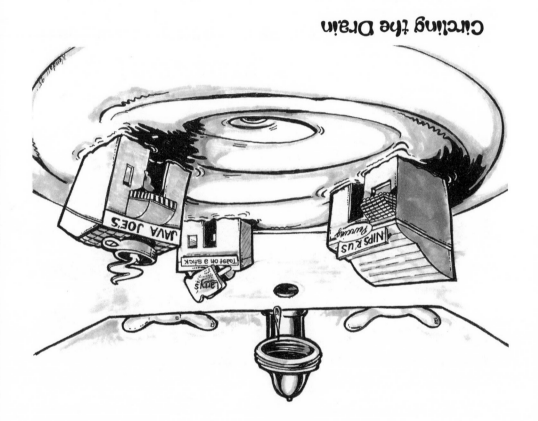

"dance music." Club music has survived for a decade. Another contender is Hi N.R.G., a fast, cheerful style, first heard in gay San Francisco clubs in the early 1980s.

Clydesdale
A stud; a good-looking guy.

Cob
Not cool; stupid.

Cobain, Kurt
The lead singer of Nirvana and the grunge movement who died an early death by his own hands (see **Nirvana**).

Cock Diesel
Buffed-out guy.

Coffee
Universal drug of choice for much of Gen X, though many have never tasted simple coffee. Gen X'ers sip mochas, double lattes, and espressos at sidewalk cafés.

Complaint Rock
Music that whines about social, economic, or environmental problems while failing to offer a resolution or encouragement. Not the same as pointing out social ills. This tendency has kept alternative rock from finding a broader audience. Tedious stuff.

Con Spirito
Lively music with spirit. The description can carry over to anyone willing to set aside the double latte and go live life to its fullest.

Contemporary Christian Music
Actually not a musical style, but a message in music. The musical form resembles current mainstream styles, including hard rock, country, and hip-hop. Every so often, a performer such as Amy Grant soft-pedals the message and reaches a broader audience. Soundscan, which tabulates sales for *Billboard's* charts, is installing scanners in Christian bookstores.

Cool Beans
An expression of moderate joy. When someone offers to pay your way into a movie, you can reply "Cool beans!" If they offer to donate a kidney to save your life, a more enthusiastic response is warranted. It is not an expression that thrives on over-use.

WHAT DEFINES A GENERATION, ANYWAY?
(continued from page 37)

parts. The first part offers a time-based definition: A generation is the group of people born within a certain time span. Simple enough, but how do we determine what that time span is? They define a generation's time span as the time it takes for that generation to reproduce and get the next generation started. They see this as eighteen to twenty-four years, but take the average, twenty-one years, as a preliminary benchmark.

This still leaves a lot unanswered. Assigning a generational label to every other decade seems pretty haphazard. This is where the second part of their definition, the "peer personality" theory, comes in. While each generation contains a great diversity of people, people within a generation share certain common experiences that have shaped their perceptions of the world. Boomers remember the Kennedy assassinations. Generation X'ers remember when the space shuttle *Challenger* exploded. Boomers remember the *Challenger* too, but their past experience causes them to see it in a different context. Simplified, this theory sees distinct peer personality characteristics that mark different generations. Taken in greater detail (*Generations* runs over 500 pages) this theory gives a clear, useful portrait of the various generations of American people.

Cop a Squat
Sit down.

Counter-cultural Zines
Small press; independently owned magazines that attempt to move beyond the single-voice, consumer-exploitation agenda of Corporate Amerika.

Crack on Someone
To criticize.

Crash Worship
A band like no other, a collective of musicians/pagans whose shows are more akin to spectacular events involving fire, naked dancing, massive rhythms, and hedonistic abandonment. They refer to themselves as the original shamans (see page 17).

Creep
To cheat on one's spouse or significant other.

Creepers
Thick-soled black shoes suitable for sneaking back into your home after a night out cheating (see above).

Crest
To smile. An example of how a brand name (in this case, Crest toothpaste) can become part of the language.

Crew
A gang; the people you hang out with.

Crib
Home; apartment; house.

Critical/Crit
Cool.

Crusty/Crusties
Dreadlocked hippie kids or punks who don't bathe and are always bumming for spare change or dumpster diving for their next meal (see **Alley Scoring**).

Crying Game
The girl is actually a boy, who makes a pretty interesting girl. (From the movie of the same name.)

Crying Game

Cujette

Cousin; same as a homegirl, but in an Italian neighborhood.

Cujine

Male version of a **cujette.**

Curb

1) Messed up: "That boy's to the curb."

2) A skinhead term in which someone's open mouth or teeth are put on the curb and then the person is stomped in the back of the head. (Actually seen on the sidewalk outside a Kansas City club at 3:00 A.M.)

Cyber-Shamanic Rock Stars

Creators of futuristic techno- and rave-type music that embraces the latest studio production technology.

Cyberbabe

1) Featured actress in Wank Ware (digital pornography).

2) Partner or friend met on the Internet.

3) The object of lust in a Wank Ware Web page or Net download.

Cyberculture

The **Internet**-connected, computer-literate portion of the populace. Attaching the prefix *cyber-* to any word lends an air of authority. **Generation X,** especially, uses powerful computers comfortably as communication-processing creativity tools to accomplish an end, not as "new, strange" technology.

Cyberese

Technospeak by the computer savvy.

Cybergeek

A nerd who excels with computers, particularly in navigating **cyber-space.** Once simply called nerds, cybergeeks enjoy the advantage of computer savvy. As computer savvy grows mainstream, however, the term is losing distinction.

Cyberia

A book, subtitled *Life in the Trenches of Hyperspace,* by author Douglas Rushkoff. The word *cyberia* plays off the remote, not-easily-accessible, insular, neo-hippie society that has carved a new techno-logical no-man's land from within the computer culture, *a la* cyber-hood.

Cybergeek

ON THE NET

BCNU: Be seein' you

ROTFL: Rolling on the floor laughing

NAA: Not another acronym

LOL: Laughing out loud

"You know what I really like about cyberspace? The rumors. Such as the recent so-called fact that the Vatican had been bought out by Microsoft. . . .One world, one operating system!"
Laurie Anderson, from the stage of Seattle's 5th Avenue Theater

Cyberlit

Literary genre of William Gibson, Bruce Sterling, and other writers of the purple rage.

Cybernetics

Theory that every action—mechanical or animal—triggers an information response feedback that determines the next action. Norbert Wiener of M.I.T. coined the term (from the Greek *kybernetes,* meaning "helmsman") while designing systems for World War II anti-aircraft guns. He realized that the critical component in any control system is the feedback loop that gives a controller information on the results of its actions or movements. His discoveries helped pave the way for the electronic brains we call computers.

Cyberpork

Government money flowing to well-connected contractors working on the Information Superhighway.

Cyberpunk

A science fiction genre that envisions worlds starkly non-utopian, in which characters share an intimate but uneasy accommodation with technology as portrayed in the movie *Blade Runner.* William Gibson is largely regarded as the leader of this group of young writers. Just as beatniks anticipated hippies, cyberpunks are setting the stage for a coming digital counterculture that will turn the late '90s **zeitgeist** utterly on its head. This movement-in-the-making has yet to be defined, much less named.

Cyberspace

Gibson calls it "a consensual hallucination . . . a graphic representation of data abstracted from the banks of every computer in the human system." Cyberspace is the uncharted region inhabited by all the data streams from all the computers in the universe. At the moment, we sit out on its edges. In the world of virtual reality we will enter into cyberspace. (William Gibson's *Neuromancer* [see **Neuromancer**] gives a graphic portrayal of cyberspace.)

Cyberspace Generation

Same as the **Digital Generation**, with an emphasis on computer technology, especially networked computers.

Cyberpunk

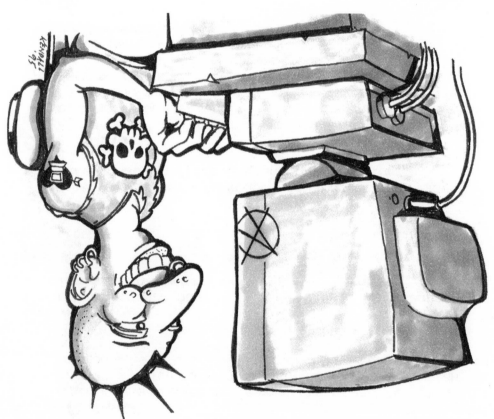

Cybertrek

Cyberspace journey to locations around the Internet and the world of networked computers. Usually a deliberate journey to relevant locations where information or software that you want is located. **Cybertrekkers** can easily get lost or sidetracked in the huge, interlaced webs of information available in **cyberspace.**

Cybertrekker

A person who spends a great amount of personal time exploring the **Internet.** Cybertrekkers can be informative guides or they can mischieviously lead the uninitiated deeper and deeper into the digital void.

Cyborg

Literally, part man, part machine. See Arnold Schwarzenegger in *The Terminator,* in which he portrays the classic cyborg.

Cybot

Cybernetic robot; a robot capable of making decisions.

Cybrarian

A person who earns a living doing online research and information retrieval. Also known as a data surfer or supersearcher.

Cypherpunk

A member of the movement to develop encryption programs enabling anyone to send secure, encoded messages via e-mail. Cypherpunks seek to make electronic privacy an inviolable right and are opposed to any government control of the **Internet.** Needless to say, some in law enforcement are opposed to them, seeing a new form of freedom of speech as a potential hotbed of electronic crime and pornography.

Da Bom

Cool.

Daddy Mac

A good-looking guy.

Daddylac

An expensive car given to a young woman or man by parents (from Cadillac).

Daddytac

Cybertrekker

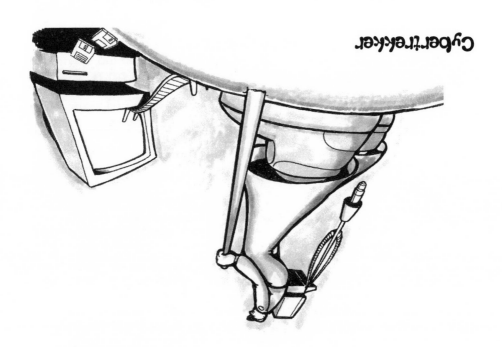

Dancehall Music to DEWKs

Dancehall Music

Speedy sing-song rapping in a Jamaican patois over a stark reggae beat spread through hip-hop and Caribbean enclaves in this country. Unlike other forms of reggae, dancehall depends more on synthesizers and sequencers than on live musicians. More importantly, DJ patter in this music style was a direct precursor of rap as we know it. Even now, East Coast rappers often dip into dancehall accents, as in Ini Kamoze's "Here Comes the Hotstepper."

Danceploitation

Taking unfair advantage of the ritual of dance by using it as an opportunity to cop a feel.

Dank, The

A type of marijuana. As in "Kind Bud" (see **Kind**).

Dead Presidents

Street lingo for money, cash.

Dead Tree Edition

The printed-on-paper version of a publication—as opposed to the electronic version. A magazine versus an **E-zine.**

Deck

The board part of a skateboard. Doubles as a bludgeon, food tray, or ottoman.

Decorate Your Shoes

To vomit.

Decruitment

A corporate euphemism for laying off workers; downsizing.

Def

Outstanding, terrific. Commonly found in rap lyrics.

Defest

The best, the coolest.

DEWKs

Dual Employed With Kids. Time-strapped and guilt-ridden, Dewks are prime targets for service providers and marketers of any product designed to enhance quality time with the kids.

Dead Tree Edition

How can you continue to justify the rape and destruction of millions
of acres of forests to print newspapers when electronic, ecologically sound news and information systems are available right now. . . .
TODAY!

Dial in on Someone to Dip

Dial in on Someone
To talk with someone; also, to metaphorically "get their number"—as in to figure out what makes a person tick, to locate all their buttons.

Digable
Cool.

Digital Generation
The Millennium Generation. The post-Gen X generation that will absorb the technology already in place to move social communication to a new level. "Digital" implies a loss of humanity as interaction and communication become less personal and more mechanized.

Digits
Phone number. "Give me your digits, I'll buzz you this afternoon."

Digizines
Magazines on CD ROM, such as *Medio* and *Blender.* The latter bills itself as a pop-culture zine covering topics from Japan's fascination with twentysomething soap operas to a guide to the most lust-inspiring areas of the **Internet.**

D/K
Dual Income With Kids. (See **DEWK.** Contrast with **DINK.**)

D/MP
Dual Income, Money Problems. A more common acronym in the credit-easy '90s.

D/NK
Dual Income, No Kids. This couple has more disposable income than the typical family. The term was first DINC (Dual income, no children), but probably changed to DINK in the mid-'80s.

Dionysian/Dionysiac Frenzy
Dionysus was the Greek God of wine and vegetation and perhaps the originator of Greek drama with the celebration of the Dionysian festival. Basis of an orgiastic religion whose ceremonies frequently ended in frenzied celebration and a breakdown of social constraints. Could be related to **raves,** a warehouse celebration that includes wine, drugs, and music.

Dip
To move fast, hurry.

EXTREME SPORTS

It's about nothing less than speed. And actions speak louder than words. The big bang theory, dirt central, extreme sports take limelight and center stage to much of the Gen X crowd. Why? How 'bout this explanation: After watching the destruction drugs had on the folks before them, the new breed seeks a rush elsewhere and turns up wind, air, speed, grind, and volume to get it.

Or they could just want to one-up the generation before? How do you go beyond? Try going faster. Longer. Harder. Crazier.

Surfing, skating and snowboarding are various styles of essentially the same activity, that being a traversal of multi-planar terrain aboard a single, plank-like vehicle. I'm talking *boards* as they are often involved—on the water, across the street, through the snow to Grandma's house we go . . . I don't think so. If not big pieces of wood then wheels: across rocky terrain on two or down sliding handrails on four. Forget those inline jobs, those are for woosies (see **Kodak Courage, Action Sports**).

The nastiest bumps, the steepest chutes, the tightest trees, speeds just shy of panic on the fear meter, grind on curbs, rails, ramps, half pipes, or go for fat air—it don't matter which one you choose, they're all related somehow, and they are all designed for abuse. Bunnyhop your lil' ol' bike across the great divide or mongo-foot that snowboard my way. Investigate your endurance limit. Push it. Push it real good.

And don't forget. These activities can all serve as energy-efficient modes of transportation or, at the very least, a vehicle for aggressive expression.

It seems these days that you pretty much have to risk your life to get anything done.

Dirt Weed to Doc Martens

Dirt Weed
Substandard commercial grade of pot.

Dis/Diss
To show disrespect; to insult; to harass. Commonly a part of **rap** culture. Most believe it was clipped from disrespect, although some insist that it is short for dismiss. Originally a term from African-American neighborhoods, dis has now become a common phrase across the cultural board in America, thanks to its dissemination by rap.

Dis and Dismiss
To have disrespect for someone and then ask him to leave.

Dismo
An intense devotee of the surfing culture who never gets his feet wet.

Displaced Nostalgia
Wistful feeling stirred by another generation's music, i.e., X'ers longing for the original music and memories of Woodstock.

Dissident Yuppie or DY
Young urban professional who does not fit the mold; a nonconforming yuppie, or as one was quoted as saying, "Yeah, I want a BMW, but I don't necessarily like them."

Ditz
Female airhead.

Doc Martens
Clunky shoes or boots, often black, which, if worn properly, confer instant alternative status. (Odd that shoes invented in 1945 should be so "in" now.) In order to ensure that people who are not legitimately alternative will have no idea what you're talking about, refer to them as Docs or DMs in the course of casual conversation. One should shudder to learn that DMs can now be purchased at Kinney Shoes. **Alternachicks** like to wear them with a dress, providing a sharply contrasting mix of style. Dr. Marten's black work boots from England are **Skinheads'** footwear of choice. Lace color can indicate affiliation, i.e., white equals white supremacy, while other colors might indicate non-racist, i.e., Skinheads Against Racial Prejudice (see **SHARPs**).

Doc Martens

Dode

A fool.

Doe

Stupid.

Does Windows

A basketball term that indicates the player can dribble, dunk, shoot from outside, guard—whatever the task—better than almost anyone else. It is also used to label a person who can perform certain tasks extremely well.

Dog

1) To intentionally ignore.

2) To criticize or bother.

3) To work hard.

4) To crumble under pressure, in skateboard lingo.

5) To have sexual intercourse.

6) To beat up.

Doin' Rips

Intense pot inhalation; pulling bong loads.

DIY

Do It Yourself. A punk rock ethos that revels in stripped-down graphics, the lack of fine polish, and the hard work of not going corporate.

Dommo

One who skateboards, surfs, or snowboards extremely well.

Dope

Cool, great.

Dreadlocks

The hairstyle most commonly associated with reggae. Originating from the Rastafarian religion's rule against cutting one's hair, it eventually spread beyond that religion and music to be worn by blacks and whites alike. A recent fad in Japan saw the youth of that nation having dreadlock extensions put in their hair as well.

THINK COURT LITE: NEW SPEEDY JUSTICE

Just as marketers are forced to examine the way Gen X'ers spend money, so are lawmakers and lawyers forced to pay closer attention to that generation's mindset with regard to politics, bureaucracy, and TV. TV?

Yep. TV. Because what the lawyers and their law-enforcing cohorts are finding are smaller attention spans courtesy of the television. Imagine for a moment an episode of *The People's Court:* in and out with only two commercial interruptions and *voila!* a decision has been reached. Even a recap has been given by an agingly attractive, small-town news reporter with a radio-friendly voice.

Now that is an overgeneralized statement, but one not without its truths. More twentysomethings have landed themselves on juries of late and their numbers are only going to increase. As they sit in that jury box waiting for the slow-moving judicial system to pick up the pace, they're looking around for the remote control. An article in *The Wall Street Journal* recently suggested putting virtual reality headsets in the jury box.

That is going to the cyber-extreme, but what can lawyers do to make the proceedings more appealing to their newfound audience? Well, one thing they're finding is a serious mistrust of authority on the part of the youth. Portraying your client as an underdog won't hurt. But the fact is, the inherent values are different from one generation to the next. In that *Wall Street*

(continued on p. 59)

Dreck

Similar to dreg, but a dreg has its place in society as a whole, while a dreck makes its name in a specific work place. "Dreck work" is the lowest task or form of labor found in a project, i.e., scrubbing toilets, law, or politics.

Dreg

Generally a human on the low end of the social food chain, a taker and abuser at the bottom of the ladder.

Drinking His Milk

Hot guy. "He's drinking his milk" (see also **Buff**).

Drop Some Iron

To spend some money.

DROPPIES

Disillusioned Relatively Ordinary Professionals Preferring Employment Situations (and a clear example of whimsical acronyms getting out of control).

Ducats/Ducketts

Money, cash. From the gold and silver coins formerly used in Europe.

Duck

Unattractive female.

Dude

Guy friend. Also a cool female friend who transcends the gender barrier. It has come to signify an almost impersonal you. The low-key, friendly greeting "Hey dude!" can be meant for almost anyone. The longer "Duuuuuuuude!" is an appreciative utterance that indicates the speaker is somewhat impressed with the behavior, spoken word, or appearance of another.

Dudical

Cool; very impressive.

DUMPIE

Downwardly Mobile, Middle-Aged Professionals.

Dutch Door Action

Bisexual activities.

THINK COURT LITE: NEW SPEEDY JUSTICE
(continued from p. 57)

Journal article, one lawyer pointed to the natural pro-American bent that jurors in the past have held. Today's younger jurors don't necessarily feel an alliance with a American company over a foreign one. They aren't necessarily as impressed with the semantics of contracts as they are by the feelings of the people involved. They tend to get just plain bored while watching the relatively staid proceedings of a courtroom.

Most Gen X'ers think *L. A. Law* when *Court TV* is closer to reality. They're looking for the dazzlingly short speeches of that television drama, not the real-life stuttering and dreary proceedings of today's courtrooms. Our advice (and *The Wall Street Journal*'s) to lawyers today is to turn on the charm. Impart the nuggets of information. Don't think for a second that facts are inconsequential. They're a necessity. Just present them attractively, dramatically, and quickly. Think breezier, think snappier. THINK COURT LITE!

Dweeb

Loser, nerd. You wouldn't want to share a locker with one.

Dystopia

Utopia's evil twin. An imaginary place that is depressingly wretched, whose inhabitants lead a fearful and bleak existence.

Dystopian

The opposite of utopian. George Orwell's *1984* and Aldous Huxley's *Brave New World* are examples of dystopia. Some have commented that the spirit of Gen X is dystopian, that there is no way out of our McWorld, so we are angry, but these negative comments have probably been used to describe other generations as they begin to assume power over their plundered country. In the case of Generation X, anger and cynicism can be healthy attributes useful to achieving national leadership.

E-Mail Terrorism

Harassed via e-mail for unpopular views or work; to become the target of persistent flames (angry diatribes) (see **Flamed**) resulting in the need to change your e-mail address. Also called Ansi Bombing.

E-Zine

Electronic magazines viewed on a computer screen. The number of **e-Zines** proliferates with the growth of the World Wide Web and its awesome multimedia capabilities.

Ear Candy

Sounds that are pleasing to the ear, often created electronically.

Earl

To vomit.

Easter Eggs

Innocuous and usually funny electronic trapdoors created by programmers of commercial software. Triggered by secret combinations of keystrokes, these "eggs" range from cartoons to surprise snapshots of the programmer's family.

Eat Chain

Drop dead; short for "Eat a chain saw."

Eat the Cookie

To get unmercifully tossed around by a wave while surfing.

Dystopia

BLADE RUNNER
A movie that presents a dark prediction for the future, a dystopia. The environment has been degraded to such a degree that there is no difference between night and day; a toxic mist falls; competition has reached its final and inevitable logic, war for valuable and scarce resources; the rich live in high-security buildings that resemble modern pyramids, and live life as if they were divine. The poor live a dystopian existence on the street in hollowed-out, lifeless buildings. There are two languages, the language of the streets and the language of the wealthy.

Ecchsters to Express

Ecchsters

An unflattering characterization of Gen X'ers in the 1994 book *Generation Ecch* by Jason Cohen and Michael Krugman.

Eco-Villain

1) An organization or person who harms the environment.
2) Ironic reference to corporations that voice concern over the environment while secretly polluting it or funding anti-environmentalist political candidates.

Ecstasy/Extasy

The designer drug MDMA, an hallucinogenic cocktail akin to a mild LSD compounded with high-density crank. Ironically, MDMA was invented in 1917 as an appetite suppressant and took over seventy years to find its niche as a recreational substance. "E" causes a potentially dangerous false sense of well-being, long-range alertness, and intense sensual fervor, inspiring the X-clamation of utterances like "My clothes! They're killing me!" and "I can feel my hair growing!" Taking the drug is called X'ing. The drug was outlawed in the United States in 1987. It has been known to cause death.

Edutainment

Software that combines entertainment with learning.

Egosurfing

Scanning the **Internet,** data bases, print media, or research papers for mentions of your own name.

Ennui

Experience of emptiness, boredom and meaninglessness. For Gen X, ennui has heightened meaning (see pp. 63 and 95).

Exerheads

Fitness freaks. Usually insanely vain and shallow people who believe that their buff bods excuse idiotic behavior (see p. 31).

Exobiota

Extraterrestrial life. Just watch *The X-Files* on the Fox Network to understand the Gen X and X-life connection (see p. 71).

Express

In the mood to party: "I'm express!"

Eco-Villain

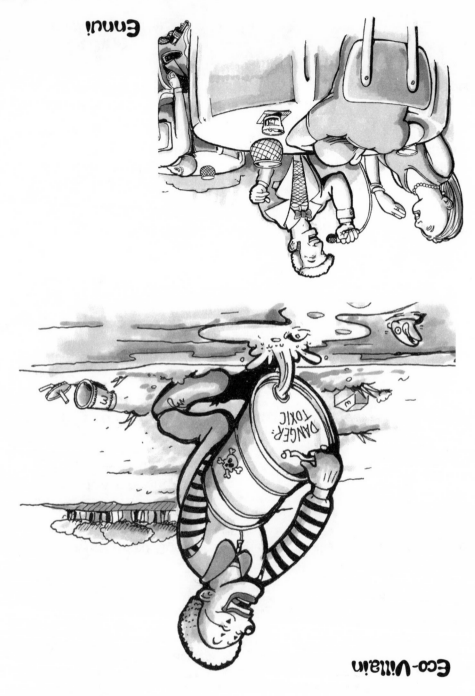

Ennui!

Eye Candy

Sights that are pleasing to the eye, especially images created on the computer's digital palette. Combine with **Ear Candy** and you get the Gen X version of a pacifier.

Eyebleeder

Pot so dense and green that it makes one's eyes water while pulling rips on a bong.

FAQ

Frequently Asked Questions—usually a file at an online site designed to eliminate repetitive inquiries.

Faced

1) Put down; having lost face.

2) Drunk, as in shit-faced.

Fan It

To pass on an offer or opportunity. Shine it, forget it, let's not do it; pass. "Let's fan on that."

Fanzine

Merge fan with magazine. The result is a puffy, uncritical periodical dedicated to a specific artist, actor, musician, or interest. Fanzines are glorifiers of their subjects.

Fat/Phat

Nice; good; cool.

Feeb

Incompetent (from feeble). "I'm a total feeb when it comes to romantic relationships."

Fictional Imagery

An advertising lie/false tale slickly and persuasively presented in an attempt to direct the targeted market victim away from the truth (see p. 69).

Filler

A relationship sustained while waiting for the right one to happen along.

Fine as Wine

Extremely attractive.

Eye Candy

Fiscal Abuse to Fly Gear

Fiscal Abuse
The selfish mortgaging of future generations by continuing the U.S. federal deficit. Increasing the multitrillion-dollar debt to fund programs now and expecting future generations to worry about paying it off.

Flag a Class
To skip a class in school.

Flag Bait
Voters who are easily swayed by politicians who wrap themselves and their agendas in the Stars and Stripes to get the vote.

Flail
To do poorly or fail a test; to mess up badly.

Flake
1) To miss an appointment, engagement or date. "She flaked out on our date."

2) To get weird on someone, to have a nervous breakdown.

Flamed
To receive a vicious diatribe via e-mail. The distance and anonymity of the Internet have emboldened many people to articulate anger in ways they wouldn't have dared in face-to-face social discourse. The fashionableness of flaming suggests it shouldn't be taken too personally. Digitally dissed.

Flavor
To have a style.

Flex
When you have to depart. "Gotta flex, man. See ya."

Fly
Fresh, dope, stupid, cool—a piece of '80s hip-hop slang that has gone totally white bread. "That new mall is so fly, dude!"

Fly Boy/Fly Girl
Attractive young man/woman.

Fly Gear
Exceptionally fashionable clothing.

FISCAL ABUSE

Like a sci-fi creature that feeds on waste and greed, Debtzilla grows with each passing moment.

It's more now, but not too long ago, America's national debt was $5 trillion dollars—enough to pay Michael Jordan's salary for two million years—and it's growing $11,000 a second, $40 million an hour, 1 billion dollars a day.

Fly Honey to Fresh

Fly Honey

A good-looking girl.

Flyer Design

Flyers are the main mode of promotion for punk rock, raves and ultra-alternative rock happenings. The design of a band's flyers should reveal its essence (see **Raves**).

Folx

Mom, Dad, Sis, Bro, and all the other family appendages.

Formica Daydreamers

Contented middle-classers who emulate *The Brady Bunch* in their enthusiasm for common denominators and their penchant for mediocrity while reveling in the unexamined life.

Fourth Wall

1) The invisible boundary between performers and audience. Breaking down the fourth wall means achieving a total connection between audience and performer. When the process (cameras, sound stage, director, and audience) becomes part of the action on stage, as frequently happened on *The Garry Shandling Show*, the fourth wall is eliminated.

2) Any barrier to understanding or appreciating, i.e., a person who doesn't listen.

Freak

1) To get excited, filled with wonder.

2) An attractive woman who is sexually permissive. "Hey man, I heard she is a freak!" "You heard wrong, dude. She's my wife!"

Fred

Geek (see also **Dweeb**). For example, a bicyclist Fred usually wears K-Mart cotton shorts (too short), T-shirt, tube socks, and generic tennis shoes. The Fred does wear a helmet, but usually it is an old V1 Pro, or a hockey or mountain-climbing helmet. There is something about the Fred that suggests he cannot transcend himself, that Fredliness is inherent, an essence, or perhaps genetic—a Fred chromosome. Of course, there is a lingering fear or suspicion that, in the end, we might all be Freds in one way or another.

Fresh

Cool, good, great, nice.

FICTIONAL IMAGERY

Cigarette companies are targeting the X generation. Philip Morris invented a new tobacco company under the cover of a corporate paper trail. This fictional company is supposedly owned by a down-home guy named Dave. Dave has taken on the big tobacco companies and their fast-burning cigarettes. Dave offers "home-grown smokes." Their manager of media affairs says that Philip Morris is not trying to deceive anyone. "It's a tale of fictional imagery,"she says. But PM has been telling its outlets not to put Dave too close to other PM brands! Nothing, we guess, would interrupt a good "tale of fictional imagery"like the truth.

Frosted

1) Cold and emotionless.

2) Angered.

FRUMPIEs

Formerly Radical, Upwardly Mobile Persons.

Full-on

Wholeheartedly. "The party was a full-on rage."

Full-on Honky Handshake

A standard computer protocol that permits peripheral equipment to connect without a lot of manipulation or complicated configuring.

Fun Tickets

Money, cash. "Can't make happy hour, Bro. I'm all out of fun tickets."

Fundage

Money, cash; bank.

Fundies

Fundamental Christians.

Funk

Type of music pioneered by George Clinton and James Brown. Some white bands, such as the Red Hot Chili Peppers, have adopted this sound from the black community.

Funkadelic

The name of George Clinton's band and his particular brand of funk— a mix of R&B, soul, rock, psychedelia, and other-planet perceptions. Funkadelic enjoyed a revival with the heavy sampling of Clinton's music by rap artists such as Dr. Dre (see **Sampling**).

Future-Proof

1) Any technology that supposedly won't become outdated.

2) An idea or concept that is timeless.

Future Towns

Emerald cities where the Wizard of Oz and his disciples hide and work their electronic magic. Shining, mirrored, paneled boxes are

(continued)

Exobiota

grouped around new-cars-only parking lots bearing names that could only have been created by a faulty printer cable connection: Ciba-Geigy, Pfizer Hoechst.

Fuzz Box

1) Musical device used by lead guitarists to make a distorted or fuzzy musical sound. Sonic Youth exemplifies the use of fuzz-box rock.

2) Used to imply a disregard for classic rock and emphasizes a preference for punk rock.

Fuzzing It Up

Digitally distorting the sounds of notes played on an electric keyboard or synthesizer. Throwback to some '80s-era pop music.

G

Gangsta (see **Gangsta**).

GQ

Stylish and good looking (from *Gentlemen's Quarterly* magazine).

Gack

A slimy person; pond scum.

Gangsta

1) A person in an inner-city gang.

2) A particularly aggressive form of rap, rooted in the real or imagined lifestyles of street-level gangsters. Macho as hell, with a serious contempt for women and a fondness for guns, cars, booze, and dope, gangsta rap lyrics provoked a congressional probe in 1994. As entertainment, this music sells more to suburban white youth than to the people it ostensibly portrays. Maybe that's what got Washington worried. . . .

Ganja

Marijuana, originally a word from India. It comes to the United States via reggae.

Gank

To steal. To get ganked is to get ripped off.

BABY BOOMERS OFFSTAGE

Though they have grown older, with sagging bodies and aged voices, Baby Boomers refuse to acknowledge that their time at stage center has past. But we are about to pull the plug on their amplifiers and push them offstage into the Mosh Pit.

Theirs was the generation of unlimited expectations, for whom anything was possible. But this mentality of unlimited possibility has come to be an incredible burden as it confronts reality. Everyone imagined that they could get the "standard package" for the American Dream: B.A. degree, good job, nice house, and family. They assumed that the attainment of this dream would be fulfilling. But fulfillment stayed elusive, always out of reach. And then came disillusionment over the Vietnam War, the decline of the economy, racial and political strife, and a host of other unpleasantries descended upon Boomers.

Garage Pop

This is solid, punkish, and usually affable music made by working-class Joes in their garages with their friends. Sometimes this succeeds and crosses over. Beck's song "Loser" is a prime example. In most instances, garage popsters are lo-fi kings. They don't use a lot of expensive equipment; they don't spend a lot on recording, but they maintain credibility, which is more important than super-produced sounds. But in this deceitful era, there are big money, major-label bands who will pay millions to get "that lo-fi sound" because that's what is selling this week. They may get that sound, but they definitely do not get "it."

Gat

Gun (from Gatling gun).

Gearhead

Motorcyclist; someone who likes motors; a hot-rod enthusiast. Sometimes so obsessive as to ignore danger and the possibility of personal injury.

Geed

Looking good.

Geek/Geek-A-Mo

A fool.

Geek Chic

Nerd style is in: orange, butterfly-collar shirts of polyester; wood-shop safety glasses; corrective shoes. Geek chic should be attempted only by the extremely good looking with the ability to make madras golf pants look fashionable.

Geek Lore

Demeaning and humiliating tales of Freds and Geeks (see **Fred** and **Geek**) who try to transcend their lot in life. For example, consider the bicyclist Fred who bought an expensive mountain bike, then never pumped up the front air shocks.

Geeklified

Made to look foolish, ridiculous.

Geeky

A fashion disaster compounded by arrested social development.

Gearhead

Gel

1) To calm down.

2) To hang out.

Gelled

Hung over; coming off an intense drug; weak.

Gender Bender

A person whose actions and appearance make gender determination difficult. Sometimes a mind-boggling decision. Consider *Saturday Night Live's* "Pat."

Generation X

1) Those born between 1960 and 1981. A generation characterized by the lack of a specific identity or role (other than that of consumer) within the larger society. The designation was popularized in a book of the same name published in 1990 by Douglas Coupland.

2) A 1960s English paperback about sex, drugs, and rock 'n' roll.

3) At one time, the name of Billy Idol's band.

Generic

Really stupid; dull; out of it.

Gentrification

The colonization of marginal ethnic neighborhoods by urban pioneers. Consequently, the original residents are forced to move away as taxes and rents skyrocket.

Get Faced

To become extremely intoxicated.

Get Moded

To be caught or humiliated.

Get Naked

A way to say "let's go." Contrary to what it, at first, seems.

Get The Net

1) To understand.

2) To be knowledgeable about the latest **Internet** tools and concepts.

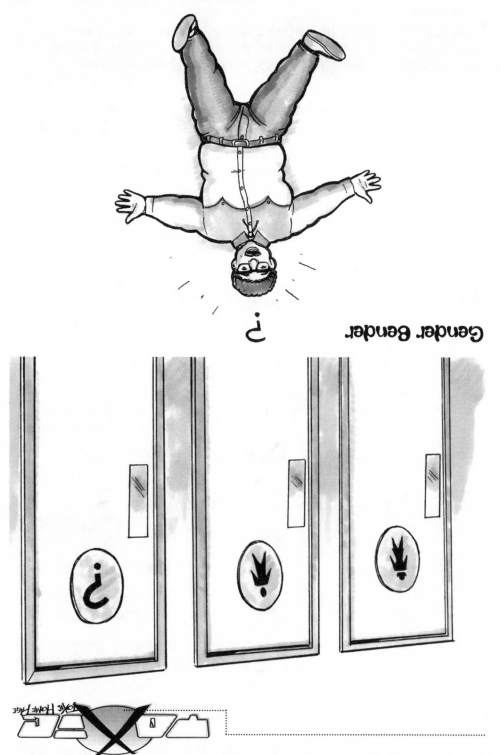

Gender Bender

Get Your Boogies On
To dance hard.

Getting Off with Your Bad Self
Gloating. Feeling obviously good about an accomplishment.

Getting Taxed
Losing money.

Getting Snapped
Caught by the law.

Ghetto Sled
Large automobile, such as a Cadillac Seville (see **Hooptie**).

Gigundo
Way large; bigger than anticipated, more than you can handle.

Glam Metal
Late '80s rock bands characterized by big hair, shiny spandex pants, eye makeup, androgyny, and loud formulaic heavy-metal or arena rock. It has strong appeal among young teenage girls. The group Poison typified this fad style of music, and the term is nearly always derogatory.

Glam Rock
A sad and dead vein of music that relied on weepy, clichéd, utterly loveless ballads; sappy, misogynistic, trite, nursery-school-level rhymer rockers about cars, bars, and stars; and a thoroughly misguided fashion sense, involving poodle haircuts, bicycle pants, cheap and cheesy leather clothes, makeup, chains, etc. All these, combined with feeble-minded posers, make up your average Glam Rock band.

Glams
The graying, leisured, affluent middle-aged; the "Got-mine, screw-yous."

Glitterbag
Women given to flashy, shiny clothes, big hair, and gum chewing.

Global Zeitgeist
The overall mood of the world. Once an inconceivable notion, the global zeitgeist is now measured nightly on the evening news. CNN broadcasts a continuous zeitgeist update 24 hours a day. Mankind

(continued)

Glam Rock

once acted regionally or locally. Now, even the smallest actions have global ramifications. **Zeitgeist** is a German word comprised of *zeit* ("time") and *geist* ("spirit"). Literally, the spirit of the time, the intellectual and moral trend of an age or period.

Gnarlatious
Fantastic.

Gnarly
1) It's good, that's great; as in, "That's gnarly, dude."

2) Difficult, challenging.

Goin' Off
Australian expression for the state of **manic nirvana** that comes at only the best rock gigs, when band and audience cross from frenzy to total jubilant obliteration.

Golden
Righteous; special; bitchin'.

Gonzo
1) Outrageous; indulging in crazed, out-of-control behavior. Though it probably developed from several sources, the "gonzo journalism" of Hunter S. Thompson, who involved himself directly in every story he covered (frequently stoned out of his mind, as depicted in his book *Fear and Loathing in Las Vegas*) spurred its current popular adoption.

2) In hacker slang it can mean very large.

Goob/Goober
Fool.

GOOD Job
A Get-Out-Of-Debt job. A job you take to pay off your debts, and one you'll quit as soon as you're solvent. (Rumored to exist, but verification is difficult.)

Gopher
A search engine, often called a softbot, which goes out into the Internet to collect, connect, sort, and retrieve specifically requested files. Archie, Veronica, and Jughead were popular search tools in the early '90s.

RAW NEWS/ON-LINE AWARENESS

There must have been a time when the misdeeds and horrors of civilization were not instantly flashed in front of our eyes as they occurred. Unbuffered and unfiltered to produce maximum shock value, they are right in our face. Just another item we have grown up with and learned to deal with.

In old film clips and history books, we see fatherly-looking nightly newscasters personally telling each viewer the "news they needed to know." Viewers looked up to these tube heroes who carefully chose the events presented, interpreted them, and then reassured viewers that things were still all right and that they could sleep well that night.

But those days left when CNN first lit up that electric glass window found in every home. Now it's all right there in our face, raw and bloodied. We interpret it, ignore it, store it away, deflect it, but it's our individual perception and choice. It makes us more world-wise. We know the world isn't a safe, secure place for us. We have to take care of ourselves.

If, to older generations, we appear to be untrusting and skeptical, **THEY ARE CORRECT.** Let them earn our trust, if they can, but we are not counting on them to take care of us. The old writing on the wall is now instant digital graffiti that would make any person of reasonable intelligence skeptical.

But we have learned well, and though we are skeptical of the motives and abilities of older generations, governments, and Corporate Amerika, we have faith and optimism in our abilities to survive and find ourselves.

And we still plan on having a good time . . . which is what it's really all about.

Granola

Anyone who dresses and shares the preferences for the flower-child culture of the 1960s.

Granola Punk

A hybrid culture of punk rock music and hippie diet/lifestyle. Granola punk bands usually wear very old **Doc Martens** or Timberland boots, scruffy flannels, and jeans. They don't eat meat. They don't do non-hallucinogic hard drugs. The look is Grateful Dead, but the sound is Pennywise and Fugazi. This juxtaposition of lifestyles can result in some interesting followings for these types of bands: headbanging hippies, violent vegans, and skinheads who hate people but think cows are sacred.

Grape Smuggler

Bikinis worn by old men at the beach (see also **Bikini Hammock**).

Graybar Land

The place your mind travels to as you stare at the computer screen, waiting for some function to finish processing.

Gremlin

Novice surfer.

Grill

Your face. From the grill on a car. "How'd you get that scrape on your grill?"

Grind

Chow-down; eat; masticate.

Grit

Cigarette.

Grobbling

Complaining.

Grommet

A young teen surfer.

Groove Jazz

Modern jazz that relies on low-end grooves as a backbone.

Granola Punk

Grumpies

Grown-Up, Mature People.

Grunge

Music identified with **Kurt Cobain** and **Nirvana** that became known as the Seattle sound during the late '80s and early '90s. While grunge had its share of fakes (like Stone Temple Pilots) and wannabes, it mercifully pulled the plug on brain-dead, big-haired heavy metal bands, which almost balances the faux grunge avalanche launched by the media in the early '90s.

Grunge Hoax (New York Times)

On November 5, 1992, the *New York Times* published an exhaustive look at grunge that included a list of grunge slang provided by a young record-company sales rep. She lived in Seattle, so the *Times* assumed she was a grunge authority. They were not amused when it turned out she was kidding; terms like *harsh realm* and *wack slacks* were her own humorous invention. Strangely, some of these terms infiltrated the common vocabulary despite their original lack of authenticity.

Grunged-out '90s

Flannel, flannel, flannel. Wardrobe and mindset augmented by second-hand clothing store threads.

Guidette

A female **guido** (see below), likely to wear big hair, tight skirts, high heels, and gobs of makeup.

Guido

Male with slick hair, gold jewelry, a hairy chest, acid-washed jeans, and an affinity for Bon Jovi music. Originally, a stereotype of Italian-American "cool," guidos are now found in any group. For example, Greek, Jewish, and Chinese guidos.

Gutter Wear

Very hip, punkish clothing.

Gutterpunk Girls

Teenagers with lots of mascara and torn jeans, usually affecting an image rather than living a lifestyle.

SPENDING THEIR INHERITANCE

Most Boomers and Silents think it's amusing to see the "We're Spending Our Children's Inheritance" bumper stickers on RVs and fancy cars.

These are the same people who whine about deterioration of the family unit and family values.

Don't they see the contradiction?

The sticker says "I've got mine, to heck with you and yours. . . . I don't care what happens to you, just keep working to pay for my entitlements."

"Christmas is a time when kids tell Santa Claus what they want and adults pay for it. Deficits are when adults tell the government what they want—and their kids pay for it."

Richard Lamm, former governor of Colorado

Hacker to Headbanger

Hacker

1) A type of computer zealot who, among other things, has learned to gain entry to other people's computer networks and sometimes tries to discover sensitive information by poking around.

2) One who enjoys the intellectual challenge of creatively circumventing limitations.

3) One who plays Hackey Sac.

Hair-a-Noid

Paranoia of the hair. Constantly checking one's hair in every reflective piece of glass one passes, be it in store windows, car windows, etc. Fear of a bad hair day or future investments in Rogaine.

Ham

Any alcoholic beverage.

Hang

1) Able to keep up or stay with; being able to do something the rest of the group or clique is doing. As in "we were on the twelfth tequila shot, and Billy couldn't hang past ten."

2) To associate with or be in the company of friends.

Hangin'

The act of socializing.

Hardcore Techno

A more aggressive form of techno that incorporates elements of speed metal and **industrial music.** It has led to some audience crossover of those genres.

Harsh Realm

The daily struggle to survive in a world where good paying, secure jobs are all but impossible to obtain, where social and economic powerlessness and uncertainty make optimism a difficult challenge. Though mentioned in the Grunge Hoax, this term is authentic (see **Grunge Hoax**).

Headbanger

Heavy-metal fan, usually teen boys with long hair and black T-shirts bearing the stylized name of their favorite bands. The name comes from a combination of early slam dancing and the frantic head-bobbing, air-guitar motions of heavy-metal fans as they emulate their on-stage heroes.

Hacker

Hacker Culture
Mixture of the independent
spirit of the counter-culture
with the rigor of engineering.

Hearse Someone

To kill someone.

Heavy Metal

Fast, harsh, and loud rock. If one of those is missing, it ain't heavy metal. Early metal influences include Led Zeppelin and Black Sabbath. In the late '70s and early '80s, the most influential bands were AC/DC, Van Halen, The Scorpions, KISS, Iron Maiden, and Motorhead. In those years, heavy metal grew to be a terribly theatrical spectacle. In the '90s, Anthrax, Slayer, Metallica, Megadeth, Skid Row, Morbid Angel, and Guns & Roses ruled the genre.

H'ed

Strung out on heroin. (Pronounced aitched.)

Hemp-chic

Cool items associated with marijuana; or clothing made from hemp fiber.

Hep Cat

A swing enthusiast. A person with a penchant for circa 1940s clothes, music, and lingo. "Hep Cat" dates back to the early 1940s and is enjoying one of its periodic revivials both in usage and style.

Hep Soho

Applies to someone who is more consumed with the insincere consumption of art and literature than with material pursuits.

Hepness/Hipness

The standard by which all hip people/trend-setters judge others and judge themselves. Another 1940s extract.

Heroic

The old-time hero fights the bad guy, gets the girl, and lives happily on his twenty acres. Today, the heroic act is defined as living through each day, working very hard, and hopefully having a job and a place to live at the end of each day.

Hip

Cool, in the forefront of style (as it has always meant).

Hip Code

Fashionable zip code, i.e., Beverly Hills, 90210.

Heroic

Hip-Hop

One of numerous variations of rap, but actually closer to describing the **B-boy** culture of dance, music, art, poetry, and DJ cut and scratching. The music focuses on a dance beat and borrows breaks shamelessly from nearly every other form of music.

Hippy Witch

A girl who dresses in black '60s-style clothing.

Hipster

An ultra-cool person. One who knows the latest and coolest in language, dress, music, art, and literature. Often a terrifically interesting person afflicted with a **gonzo** ego.

Holmes/Homes/Homie/Homey

Derivations of **homeboy/homegirl** (which mean the same thing); a common rap term.

Holy Wars

Perpetual electronic bulletin board debates over subjects like abortion, gun control, and Macintosh versus IBM.

Homeboy/Homegirl/Homeperson

Usually a friendly term of address for someone from the same neighborhood or school; a neighborhood friend.

Homepage

An Internet document created with HTML (HyperText Markup Language) (see **HTML**) that contains text, graphics, and links to other homepages found on the World Wide Web. With the ease of use of HTML and the popularity of the Web, many individuals are creating their own homepage as a means of introducing themselves to the world, prompting a revision of Andy Warhol's prediction: In the future, everyone will get their fifteen megabytes of fame on the Web.

Honk

To vomit.

Hood

Neighborhood.

Buzz Bin

Hook

The part of a song that is the most memorable, whether it be the lyrics or the melody. The part that grabs you.

Hookie

A college student who espouses apathy and noninvolvement. Derived from "Who cares?" The University of Utah, an apparent hotbed of political apathy, attracted press attention in 1988 because of its large Hookie population.

Hooptie

Big gas-guzzling cruiser with a minimum one thousand square feet of interior. Suitable for those unplanned, homeless odysseys or as a spare bedroom for uninvited house guests. Achieves old motorboat effect when accelerating; also a highway tank. Frequently a dinosaur Olds 88.

House Music

Early '80s form of party music that originated in Chicago when DJs began to combine European electronic pop, like Kraftwerk, with soul and funk albums by George Clinton's Funkadelic along with beats from their own programmable drum machines. This upbeat-sounding music led to **Acid House.**

HTML

HyperText Markup Language. The code used to create World Wide Web pages.

Huffers

Devotees of low-budget highs induced by a wide variety of readily available, legal substances. These include glue, solvents, and aerosol propellants. Pressurized cans of air used to clean out computers and other appliances are particularly popular. Huffing is usually an activity for the young, whose access to other drugs is limited, or for desperate types who'll take any high they can find.

Hum

To stink. "This place hums."

Huppie

A blend of hippie and yuppie. Describes a person who is upwardly mobile but spends his spare time living unconventionally in the manner of a hippie.

Hooptie

Hyper-inanity

Psychobabble; too much, too fast, with too little sense. Just because information can be delivered at the speed of light does not necessarily mean people want to hear it, or that it is worth anything.

Hypertext

The interconnection of texts on the **Internet** through key words (usually highlighted in a different color) imbedded in the document. World Wide Web pages with related information are frequently interconnected this way. Individuals with their own Web page often hyperlink collections of their favorite pages as a way of sharing. Web cruisers often revel in the nonlinear discovery process as they jump from link to link, never sure of their destination.

Ice

Smokable crystal methamphetamine, the speed freak's equivalent of crack. Incredibly potent, it never quite caught on as extensively as Drug War alarmists feared (one puff would addict you immediately, some claimed), but it's still out there.

Iconographic Sound

Music that symbolizes something special to its listeners, or takes on added depth of meaning on a personal level for various reasons, as **Nirvana's** music did after **Kurt Cobain's** death.

Iconography

Experimental visual forms, pictures.

Illin'

Stupid, un-chillin'; a common rap music term.

Indie Band

Independent band. Conventional major record labels support their bands with bountiful advances that are really just no-interest loans. Bands that shun the major labels and either go with a smaller record company or forego the support entirely and record and release their album themselves are considered Indie. Virtually all the Indie labels, the small, garage-grown companies, are being bought up by the majors, but are still retaining their Indie name, making the true Indie band a distant reality.

MILLENNIAL ENNUI

If Beckett's *Waiting for Godot* were written today, it might go like this: The setting . . . Beckett's barren landscape has been replaced with a decaying mall built in the late '70s. A single tree, surrounded by concrete, is the only indication that nature had ever held sway here. Sean and Dylan, two employees of stores that have gone out of business, loiter beneath the tree, their tattered work suits revealing Green Day T-shirts and hitched-up Calvin Klein underwear beneath. Although they stand next to each other, they converse on cellular phones, in tones strangely reminiscent of Beavis and Butthead.

S: Everything's wasted but the tree, dude.
D: This sucks. Wait—I got an idea! Let's waste ourselves!
S: Cool. But with what?
D: You forgot the rope again, you loser?
S: Whatever.
D: Wait . . . check it out. My belt's hanging from this tree.
S: Yeah, but it's too short.
D: You could grab onto my legs.
S: Yeah, right. In your dreams, pervert. Besides . . . who'd grab onto me?
D: Whatever.
   [They both grab the belt and it snaps in half.]
D: This sucks big time. I can't cope with this crap anymore!
S: Oh well. We can waste ourselves tomorrow.
D: Great. Something to look forward to. Maybe we'll get on the news.

ENNUI AND SUICIDE

Wataru Tsurumi has written a book for Japan's Generation X: *The Complete Manual of Suicide.* It has sold over 200,000 copies, the majority of which have been to people under thirty. Tsurumi says that modern life is hopeless, a continuous repetition of meaningless activities. But could we imagine a situation where the sense of ennui was so great that the act of suicide—which is an act, even though one of despair—would be continuously delayed? Samuel Beckett pegged this concept decades ago in *Waiting for Godot* in a scene which could play for some Gen X'ers with just a few minor changes.

Industrial Music

The grinding sounds of industry and commerce merge with the compelling beats of dance and rock. Judiciously sampled (see **Sampling**) machine clanking, electronic feedback, random radio noise, and techno clunking permeate the music—conjuring the specter of a post-techno era of decay—as cyberpunk writer Gareth Branwyn observes, "the sound our culture makes as it comes unglued."

Industrial Rock

Heavy-metal guitars rise up from the twisted wreckage of sampled (see **Sampling**) industrial sounds to wage nightmarish battle. Ministry, Nine Inch Nails, KMFDM, and Skinny Puppy are good examples.

Influencia

Those who influence the actions and thoughts of large groups of people, as in intelligensia.

Infobahn

Proposed as a more cosmopolitan, global-sounding name for the Information Superhighway. As **bandwidth** improves and the speed of data transmission increases, it may just become the word of choice.

Insane

Having no fear. Willing to do just about anything for fun and excitement (see **Kodak Courage**).

Internet

The sprawling, interconnected collection of computer networks worldwide. Originally designed by the U.S. military in the event that conventional communication systems were knocked out during a nuclear attack. The Net was nurtured and maintained by colleges and universities and became a means for transmitting academic research and information. Today, with more than 20 million global users, the Internet is the humble beginning of a worldwide information superhighway that will connect every person with access to a computer or telephone.

IRC

A popular mode of communal communication, Internet Relay Chat is a program that allows Net surfers to chat with each other by typing in messages that are read and responded to right away. IRC "channels" can involve group conversations or one-on-one chat. Topics can vary, but while there are many specialized discussion groups, social contacts and sexual exchanges seem to dominate. Some brave souls have even married people they "met" on IRC.

FILE EDIT DELETE HELP Self-Destruct

BOARDING
AKA SKATEBOARDING

Skateboarding got a resuscitatin' jump start with the onslaught of Gen X'ers who got their first (big) wheels in the heydays of Tony Hawk and Christian Hoisoi. Those old pros still walk the line but the new breed of youngsters—pro, on-the-rise ams and your average street-skatin' dork—can take the spotlight on the street or in the air.

Skating takes all forms, goes anywhere. To vert or not to vert, that is the question . . . "I might skate a pool one day, a ramp one day, street skate one day, sleep for a week. . . ." It's versatility that counts. And the number of bruises you wear on your knees.

Where to skate? There is no answer. Other than everywhere. Anywhere. Every skater has trouble finding that perfect spot, and having done that, keeping it. Hit the parking garages, the industrial parks, town hall, handrails, staircases, abandoned buildings. Those few public parks built "for" skaters are just playpens: watch 'em, monitor 'em. Skating is an ingenious invention to the street freak just for the sheer fact that you can be anywhere and ride. Try uptown, downtown, out of town, in any town.

Cuts, bruises, scrapes, broken bones: notches on the belt, points in the big game. Show off your best stunts and win a trip to meet a real live judge. Like the homeless and panhandlers, skaters are sought out and unwelcome where they stand out most. The pursuit of a good time and a good challenge (virtues in their minds) are unrewarded.

Professional's names and the companies who sponsor them litter the walls of the kiddies' bedrooms. Why? Pro is an

(continued on p. 99)

Iron Pimp
School bus.

I-Way
The Internet.

Izod
Preppy girl or guy.

Jack Someone
To rob someone.

Jacked
1) Happy.

2) To have messed up.

Jacked Up
To get messed up; beat up.

Jake
To flake out (see **Flake**); to stand someone up.

Jaker
One who flakes out (see **Flake**).

Jamaican Bomber
A large Jamaican marijuana cigarette.

Jaw Jack
To talk a lot.

Je Ne Sais Quois
A pseudo-sophisticated way to describe an undefinable quality in a person or thing. Translated from the French, it means "I don't know what," which doesn't quite have the same ring to it.

Jerry Chaser
Someone who devoted much time and energy to the pursuit of the Grateful Dead; name derived from the band's late leader, Jerry Garcia. No longer a viable career option.

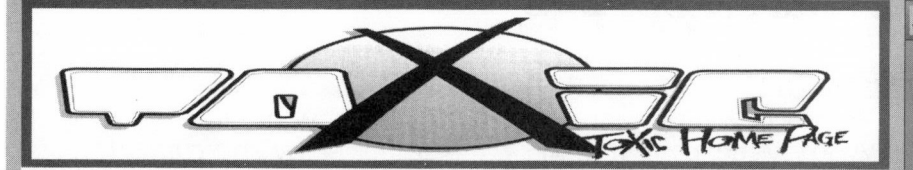

BOARDING *(continued from p. 97)*

attainable goal, it's easier than trying to get in the movies. Who needs good looks. Just the ability to fall. Hard and often.

Brian Howard, Neal Hendrix, Mike Frazier, Tony Hawk, Willy Santos, Rick Jaramillo, Matt Schnurr, Jamie Thomas, Ed Templeton, Wade Speyer, Alien Workshop, World Industries' Plan B, Deluxe, Rhythm and Planet Earth, Girl and Chocolate, Birdhouse, Hookups and Flip, Toy Machine . . .

Or the art of it all. Skater artisans like Mike Gonzales, Ed Templeton, Natas Kaupas, Jeff Tremaine have gone from producing simple logos to a vast array of highly personal graphics to real art. Art. Hell, they've even been in them big galleries and museums of late.

Skateboarding goes through its different cycles, different styles come and go, in and out. Skaters intertwine from all generations, and at contests or demos there's always a huge mix. Just like at the Board in Orange County demo or the Venice Street Grind or the Munster Championships, the oldies came out. Totally rad. The few female skaters show and it's gnarly—this huge jumble of stuff that makes it so rich. And there are older tricks that newer kids can't do, and the new tricks that fly.

Hit the street: the ollie backside noseslide, frontside fifty-fifty, fakie 180 frontside ollie, heelflip pop shove-it, the nollie flip, the nollie manual. And to the vert: the fakie and the backside kickturn, the frontside grind, the tail drop axle stall, the frontside grind. Whoa. What's it like to cross a six-foot gap four stories high, roof to roof? The hardest part is pushing toward it. You look at the other side and never think twice. The feeling of landing a twenty-stair handrail. Yeeaah! That's it! . . . except when you land square on your back.

It's all about getting up and doing it again. Going for the rush of speed and landing the nastiest, gnarliest trick. It's poetry in motion and to the skater, way better than a fat-cat paycheck.

Jheri Curl

A smelly hair substance once used, and now mostly abandoned by African Americans. It makes the hair look shiny and curly. Now, calling someone a Jheri Curl is a putdown.

Jilted Generation

Those whose birthright was squandered and mortgaged by the Boomer and Silent generations.

Jimmy

Penis.

my Cap

Condom.

Jingus

Bogus (see **Bogus**). Totally cool.

Joanin'

To insult publicly, as in "they were joanin' me about my car." When this term was reported by the *Washington Post* in 1987, it was suggested that it might be derived from Joan Rivers, but a number of readers wrote to point out that the term was an old one that was common in the African-American community back when Rivers was waiting for her first break.

Jolt Cola

A cola containing large amounts of sugar and caffeine, a backlash against the low-caffeine diet sodas of the early '80s.

Jonesin'

Badly in need of. "I'm jonesin' for a double espresso."

Jungle

A British offshoot of **techno,** now largely a separate scene that has some followers in the United States. Merging Jamaican reggae, dancehall, and ragga styles with breakbeat, Jungle is fast music frequently offset by long, slow bass lines. Jungle is a cross-cultural music that finds black and white British youth partying together despite the tensions in their society.

Juppies

Japanese Urban Professionals.

Jimmy Cap

Kevorking

To kill something. "Look, kevork that project and let's go out for a burger," or, "I read half the article, got bored, and kevorked it." From Dr. Jack Kervorkian, famous for assisting suicides.

Kick It with Someone

To spend time with someone; to socialize.

Kick Stomp

To dance.

Kickin'

To relax, usually at one's domicile. It may come from the term *kick backs*, an unearned financial reward that would usually cause one to relax.

Kicks

Shoes.

Kind

Used to describe something that is the best in its class. "The Kind," or in Hawaiian, "Da Kine."

Kinderfeindlichkeit

From German, meaning "a societywide hostility toward children." A horrific concept that takes on particular meaning given the current "fiscal abuse" of the young.

Kitsch-ridden

Maximum tacky; but kitsch-ridden art, furniture, and clothing all have an appeal for the disenfranchised. By coveting and collecting objects viewed as in bad taste by the previous standard bearers of society, one can set his or her own standards.

Knob-Twirler

A DJ at a rave or party. An expert knob-twirler can make a career out of it by doing professional remixes and the like. A knob-twirler is also a musical term for a production engineer, used when a band records. It's considered cheesy to have a producer for one's records, so said person is referred to as a knob-twirler.

Kitsch-ridden

Kevorking

Kodak Courage

An extra dose of courage and the tendency to go beyond one's usual physical limits when being filmed or photographed, especially during action sports, such as skateboarding, snowboarding, and extreme skiing (see **Insane**).(See also p. 173.)

Lamestain

1) Uncool person.

2) Put down for someone who is dull, beat, annoying, etc. They may actually leave traces of their lameness. While another piece of the infamous *New York Times* Grunge Hoax, this phrase has found its way into actual use (see **Grunge Hoax**).

Last Booty Call

Last half hour before a bar closes in the evening.

Latchkeys/Latchkey Kids

Children who are left at home alone for at least part of the day while their parents work (see page 135).

Lates

Hasta la vista, peace, later days, c'ya, good-bye for now.

Latronic

Later, good-bye.

Lay Down Tracks

Expression in the music industry referring to recording on multitrack tape.

Lay Your Cane in a Dusty Corner

To copulate. This metaphor implies the participants may be old (over 35).

Leathers

Refers to a piece of leather clothing; leather jacket, leather pants, etc.

Let Me Sex You Up

A sexual proposition. "Let's do it"; "I want to make love to you"; or "I want to have sex with you."

Lifer

Someone who is overly enthusiastic about working at a dead-end job or someone who has spent a long time slaving for a paltry wage.

Kodak Courage

Limp/Limp Out

To relax. "Let's limp out before we hit the concert." (See **Chill/Chill Out.**)

LIPS

Couples with Low Income whose Parents Support them. Coined in the wake of dinks (see **Dink**).

Liverbasher

One who takes in numerous cocktails on a daily, almost ritualistic, basis. A person who finds a special friend in the bottle.

Living Large

Doing well (in rap speak); to be very successful.

Loadies

Druggies. Always loaded, usually on marijuana.

Lo-fi

The modern incarnation of the garage-band aesthetic; its name derived from the generally inexpensive home-recording equipment used by up-and-coming **indie** bands (see **Garage Pop, Indie Band**). Established **alternative** groups also strive for this sound nowadays, a welcome reaction to the overproduced excesses of modern Top 40 drivel.

Loke

The out crowd.

Lollapalooza

A traveling music fest and vendor circus featuring MTV bands and body piercing, put together by former Jane's Addiction leader Perry Farrell in 1991. An interesting case of Gen X appropriating a slang term from a previous generation.

Loxie

A natural blonde, like Goldilocks, as opposed to a boxie, who gets it out of a bottle.

Lullaby

To kill. "We're going to lullaby that fool."

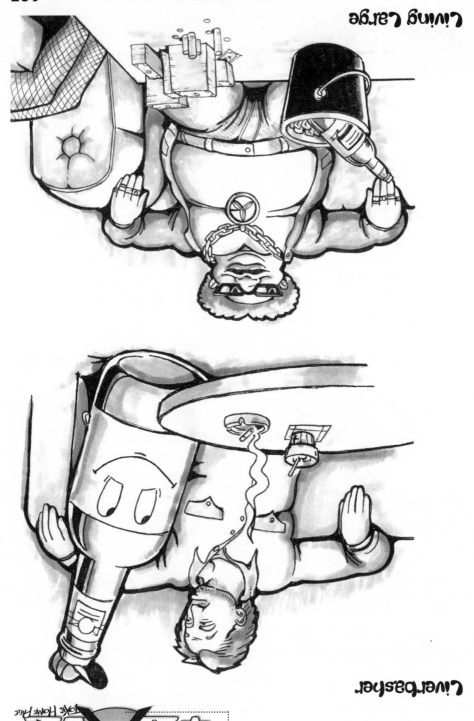

Living Large

Liverbasher

Lysergic Nudge

The rush toward activity resulting from LSD in the bloodstream.

Mac

1) To eat voraciously.

2) A cool guy.

Mac Daddy

A guy who uses women for what he can.

Macked

To get hit hard by a huge wave.

Macker

A huge wave.

Macking

Said of the ocean that is generating huge waves.

Madd

A lot of. "This place is madd with geeks!"

Maffies

Middle-Aged Affluent Folks.

Mag

1) A magazine for an assault weapon.

2) The new magazine style, such as an **e-zine,** *Pulp-Mag, Gossy, Wired,* etc.

Mainstream Mania

It's what happens when something of substance (such as **Nirvana**) or something of faddishness (flannels) goes beyond the bars and thrift stores. Suddenly these items or people are doused in media coverage and consumer dollars. When mainstream mania hits, credibility wanes.

Majorly

Extremely. "This place is majorly weird."

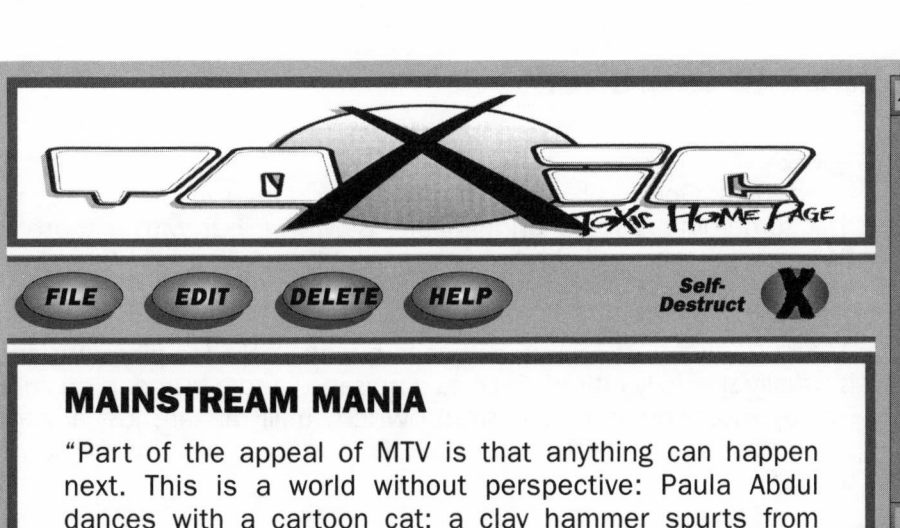

MAINSTREAM MANIA

"Part of the appeal of MTV is that anything can happen next. This is a world without perspective: Paula Abdul dances with a cartoon cat; a clay hammer spurts from Peter Gabriel's clay head; David Byrne of Talking Heads is a child one minute, a face projected on a house the next. For sixteen minutes—the network's estimate of the average viewer visit—logic takes a break."

(John Leland with Marc Peyser in *Newsweek*)

Malaise

Uneasiness. Goes with ennui and angst, and involves a vague sense that something, usually undefinable, is wrong, but with a sense of "Who cares? We can't change it anyway." (See **Angst** and **Ennui**.)

Mall Rats

A curious breed of teenager that frequents malls for pleasure, and is usually shoddily attired. Seen as a nuisance and a burgeoning criminal by most shoppers and store owners, mall rats are just a stage some slackers go through on their way to becoming twentysomethings.

Mallies

Young people who hang around shopping malls.

Manic Nirvana

Attitude, mind set, atmosphere achieved or created at a Nirvana concert. Now, unfortunately, an almost mythical state. Persons still seeking this heightened awareness are often separated from their money by the Geffen record company.

Max and Relax

To relax.

McJob

A low-pay, low-prestige, low-dignity, low-benefit, no-future job in the service sector.

McSalary

Wages one receives from working at a **McJob.** The wages are not enough to begin buying into the American dream of owning a home and making investments for the future.

McSlaves

X'ers working **McJobs** earning **McSalaries.**

Mega-

Very large or intense. Prefix of emphasis, along with **mundo-.**

Merched

The commercialization of anything, but particularly things seen as representative of Gen X. Being merched is often not a good thing. It implies that one has sold out in some sense. Whatever it is that has been merched, it then stops being itself and becomes product (see p. 179).

> ## MALAISE
>
> Who cares, but with a dose of *AngXiety.*
>
> "Something is very wrong, but why should I care?
> I have no idea what it is,
> and I couldn't change it anyway."

McJob

"Let me get this straight, we're supposed to live and work at McJob
wages to pay Social Security for these selfish fools?"

Mersh

Commercial product for mass consumption. Mick Jagger is mersh. So is McDonald's. Mainstream mania can lead a product with substance to mersh, first overexposing it, then overmarketing it, until all that is left is a mersh product.

Met Ed

Hip-hop slang for getting messED over, dissED, screwED, rippED off.

Metty-phorical

Smug interpretation of a metaphor. This term implies that it is a good thing to be educated, but not so educated that one constantly delves into metaphors and allegories instead of simply making a point.

Mick Class

Shortened version of Mickey Mouse Class. An easy class at school.

Mickey D's

McDonald's. The company now uses this name in some of its ads, which are obviously aimed at the young consumer. There are other slang fast-food names, including the B. K. lounge for Burger King and the perennial DQ for Dairy Queen.

Microserfs

1) Those enslaved in lowly servitude to Corporate Amerika during the digital ages.
2) The title of the fictional work by Doug Coupland about the Generation X'ers who actually do the work at Microsoft.

Millennial/Millennium Generation

The generation after Generation X. Also called the **Y Generation.**

Mint

Bank, fundage, money.

Modeiant

Of or pertaining to the once very popular rock group Depeché Mode.

Mondo

Extremely.

Microserfs

Moronocide
To kill all those who don't understand.

Morphs
Shapes seen when under the influence of hallucinogens. They used to be called visuals.

Mosh Pit
The floor area immediately in front of a concert stage where fans thrash around in a musically induced frenzy. It is viewed from the out-side as a whirlwind of faces, elbows, waving hands, and torsos where bodies of fearless souls are passed around overhead, floating as if on a swirling river. Circular running and body slamming occur at the center, while shoving and trampling occur farther out. A cross between some violent tribal dance and the running of the bulls at Pamplona. (Hemingway probably would have written a novel or two about it.) (See **Body Surfing.**)

Moshing
Activity of the crowd in the **mosh pit.**

MOSS
Middle-aged, Overstressed, Semiaffluent Suburbanite.

Motorhead
Influential heavy-metal band founded by Lemmy Kilmister in 1975 after he was bounced from progressive rock throbs Hawkwind. Lemmy creates aggressive, speed-freakish, lyrically incomprehensible, unwashed, biker-friendly, working-class rock—over and over. Still, the band's "No Sleep 'til Hammersmith" (1981) may be one of the best heavy metal albums ever made. Besides inspiring the next generation of speed, thrash, and **heavy metal** rockers, the band was the model for the classic comedy *Spinal Tap.*

Movin'
Cool.

MTV
Music Television, a concept that seems so natural today, was a revo-lution in 1980 when the cable channel began broadcasting the pro-motional videos produced by record labels for their new acts. MTV quickly became synonymous with youth culture, taking down '70s

(continued)

Morphed

THE GLASS NIPPLE

The picture tube—our womb

The screen—our babysitter

The cable box—our treat

The media moguls—our surrogate parents

DEATH BY MORONIC ENTERTAINMENT

rock 'n' roll as the camera sought out more visually appealing and youthful rock stars. Savvy videots with limited musical skill capitalized on the new visual paradigm. Image and music were married and not until death do they part. During its first decade, MTV championed dance pop, rap, alternative, and arena rock.

MTV Generation

1) Those kids raised on **MTV** who view the music channel as their primary source of culture.

2) Someone who came of age in the '80s and is marked by a short attention span, limited vocabulary, modest aspirations, and an icily hip attitude.

Muffie and Biff

Put down for preppies by regular high schoolers.

Mullet

A type of hairstyle favored by hicks, geeky jocks, and some female tennis stars; short on the sides, long in the back. Popularized by the rap group The Beastie Boys.

Multimedia

A computer-based collection of video, audio, text, graphics, animation, and interactivity.

Mundo-

Prefix for emphasizing that something is very strange; for example, "mundo-bizarro."

Mushmouth

1) A person who lies.

2) Drunken blather.

Nappy

Gross; nasty. "That girl is nappy."

Narcolepsy/Narcoleptic

A condition in which the victim can suddenly fall asleep in any situation. See the movie, *My Own Private Idaho*, in which River Phoenix's character is stricken with this disease. It is sometimes used as a put down—labeling the recipient as someone who is completely out of it (not intellectually conscious) most of the time.

Narcolepsy

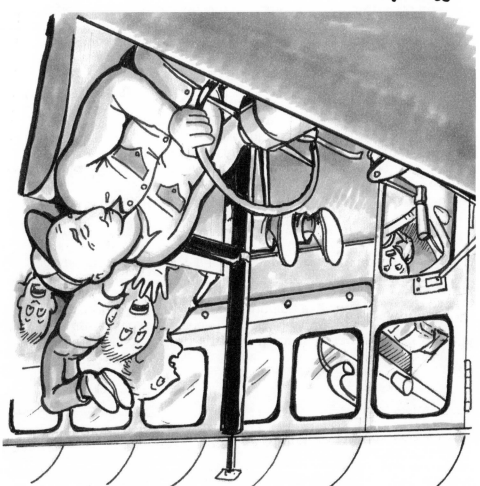

Narf

1) Bad.

2) Surprised.

3) Hello. Three distinctly unrelated meanings.

Narg

Bad; ugly.

Nectar

Beautiful.

Neologisms

Rationalizations for usually shaky theories, made to sound stable by the use of weak explanations (shored up with newly coined catch-phrases that have little or no grounding in actuality).

Net Spider

Someone who jumps frequently from one computer net site to another.

Net Surfing

Cruising through the **Internet,** looking for interesting sites.

Netiquette

Standards of behavior and conduct on the **Internet.** There is no formal code, nor a formal means of enforcement, but usually people learn proper manners in a short time.

Neuromancer

William Gibson's novel, the first to win science fiction's triple crown—the Hugo, Nebula, and Philip K. Dick awards—quickly became a cyberpunk classic, attracting an audience beyond the world of science fiction. Critics were intrigued by the dense, technopoetic prose style that invites comparisons to Hammett, Burroughs, and Pynchon. Computer-literate readers were drawn by Gibson's nightmarish depictions of an imaginary world disturbingly similar to the one they actually inhabit today (see **Cyberspace**).

New-Collar

Term created for middle-class Baby Boomers in the context of the work place. They can afford to purchase new clothing whenever they want. Also called new-collar workers.

FILE   EDIT   DELETE   HELP   Self-Destruct **X**

NEW JACK CITY
THE MOVIE, 1991

"This ain't about success, this is about survival."

"Money talks. Bullshit runs the marathon. So see ya—and I wouldn't want to be ya."
(A farewell to a cheating dealer before he is dropped head first off a bridge.)

"It's always business, it's never personal."

"You can trust me. I got yo back."

"The 'New Jack' philosophy is to 'give it to you straight, no chaser.'"
(The producer of New Jack City*)*

"You still got the gall, to try to rule. . . .But you failed the New Jack School."
(Queen Latifah, rapper)

The young male residents of Harlem are less likely to live to age 40 than the young male residents of Bangladesh—and face a higher risk of being killed by age 25 than the risk faced by U.S. troops during a full combat tour in Vietnam.

New England Journal of Medicine

New Jack City

1991 film produced by Warner Brothers that, among other things, showed the ruthlessness needed to survive in the drug-laced, gang-controlled, violent inner city, where even a momentary lapse of absolute toughness brings about death and downfall. It's become a metaphor for the ruthless survival of the fittest. Having the will and the intelligence to survive, unencumbered by societal morals/mores (see p. 119).

New Jack Swing

Music combining elements of hip-hop, R & B and old soul music.

Newbie

A new user on the **Internet.**

Nim-Rod/Nimrod

An individual that insists on turning every multiword term into an acronym.

Nintendo Wavers

Those X'ers born in the '70s.

Nip Factor

Coldness. "What's the nip factor outside?"

Nirvana

Influential alternative rock trio formed by **Kurt Cobain** and Chris Novoselic in 1986, with drummer Dave Grohl added in 1990. In 1991, with a single album, *Nevermind,* and the song "Smells Like Teen Spirit," the Seattle-based band upended the rules of rock 'n' roll. For the first time, a post-punk, alternative rock band broke out of the college radio ghetto and became a huge commercial and mainstream success. They also launched the grunge fashion movement (flannel shirts and denim). (See **Grunge.**) Cobain's deeply personal lyrics were imitated by hundreds of bands. His final lyrical statement, committing suicide on April 8, 1994, sent shock waves through the music community and beyond.

Nog

To come into contact with.

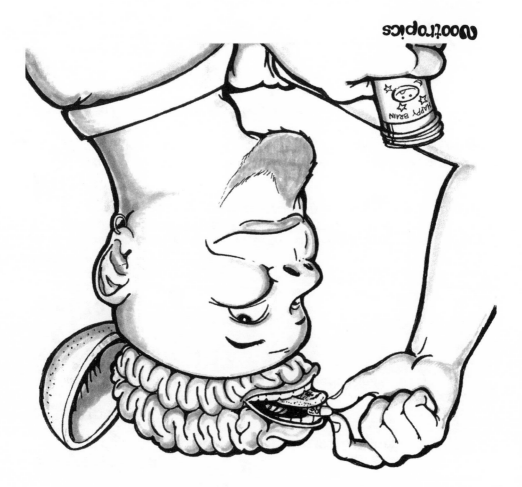

Nootropics

Noise Terrorists

A vein of music that regards melody as the enemy. An offspring of industrial (see **Industrial Music**). It is very aggressive and usually mechanized in its nature.

Noisemeisters

Record producers or record-production **knob-twirlers.**

Nootropics

Smart drugs. From the Greek term *nous* ("mind") and *tropos* ("to change"). Vasopressin seems to be a favorite (see p. 121).

Nose Nuggets

Boogers.

Nosh/Knosh

To snack.

Not!

"Not really, just kidding." A term coined from the movie *Wayne's World*. "I like your velvet shirt. . . . NOT!" Used at the end of a statement of fact, expresses denial, negation, or refusal.

NRN

1) E-mail short-hand for "No Response Necessary." Tacked to end of message, it's designed to eliminate endless back-and-forth acknowledgments.

2) Also used in personal speech to indicate "The argument is over, so shut up."

Nuck

Agreeing with someone.

Nuclear Family

The traditional "intact" family unit where mom and dad live together forever while they lovingly raise their children. Ozzie and Harriet, *Father Knows Best,* and finally *The Brady Bunch.* (see **Brady Bunch** and **Post-Nuclear Family**).

Occupational Slumming

To take employment that requires much less skill and education than one has. This is usually done to avoid responsibility and to minimize the probability of occupational failure. (See p. 125.)

Noise Terrorists

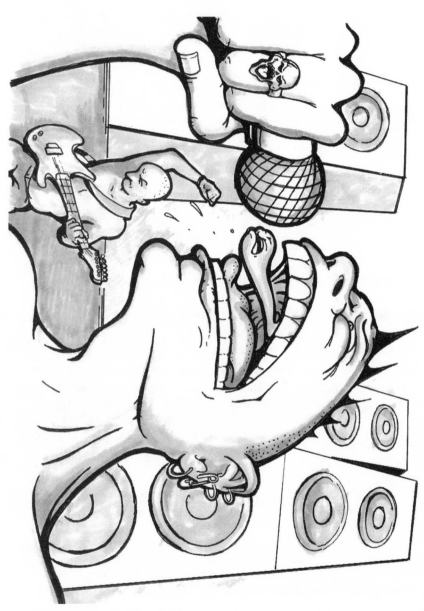

Oeuvre

A body of work; often used tongue-in-cheek about someone who hasn't done much, because someone who has actually accomplished things would have a portfolio.

Ohnosecond

That tiny fraction of time when you realize, for example, you've hit the wrong computer key and irretrievably sent your diary to an international Usenet for all the world to see.

On Hit

To be exceptional.

Onedownmanship

This is inverted bragging for those who feel it's no longer cool to have money or stability. Nowadays, the harder you had it, or have it, the more credibility you deserve. Example:

A: "When I was 14, I remember I had to get a job to help support the family when my dad got laid off by GM."

B: "Yeah, I remember when I was 12 and I had to sell my shin bones for Mom's neck-cancer operation."

B successfully onedowns **A,** making herself seem more respectable in the process.

Open-Collar Workers

People who work at home or telecommute.

Oy

Exclamation of displeasure.

Ozium

The air freshener designed to remove offensive and/or incriminating odors from your room. Also great for covering up puke or pot smell in cars.

Packing a Nine

1) Carrying a 9 mm. pistol. Gang term. The 9 mm. pistol also might be referred to by its manufacturer's name: Glock, Taurus, and Beretta being the most popular.

2) Ready and able to fight or stand up for oneself. "She came to the meeting packing a nine."

"Singing the Too Many Part-Time Jobs Blues"

Occupational Slumming

Pan-Frontiersman

One who returns to the pagan attitudes put forth by many new publications, artists, etc. This person usually has much in the way of tattoos, body piercing, and ornate hair.

Party On

Continue having a good time. From *Wayne's World.* "Party on, dude."

PC

Politically Correct. A person or group that takes great care not to offend any other group or person during a discussion. Examples include using a suffix to indicate someone with a handicap, i. e., visually challenged instead of blind (how about solvency-challenged for being broke?). People who pride themselves on their political correctness are often also concerned about the latest environmental or personal crisis in the world, such as global warming, rain forest depletion, or school lunch programs for poor families.

Peel a Cap

To fire a pistol, to shoot a bullet; almost always from an unregistered gun (See **Bust a Cap**).

Peep This

Look at this. Check this out.

Person Man

A weak warrior who gets creamed in his first battle. A failed player in a world that tolerates everything but a loser.

Petunia

A male who pays a great deal of attention to his appearance.

Phase Shifters

People who party all night and sleep all day. A term that some **ravers** use to describe how they change their relationship with the planets (see **Rave** and **Vampire Time**).

Phase-Space

A term used by ravers (see **Rave**), derived from phase locking. Perhaps this is the area between elements of a unified whole or the area where the phase takes place. It is utterly pretentious and reminds one of the drug-addled tribalism invoked by such pseudo-shamans as Timothy Leary and Terrance McKenna.

CENTER FOR THE
ETHICALLY
CHALLENGED

Politically Correct

Phat/Fat

Cool; in style; hip.

Pheenin'

Going crazy. Wigging out.

Phillies Blunt

Blunts are hollowed-out cigars stuffed to bursting with **ganja,** a process that creates a larger-than-life superdoob. A blunt in combination with a 40-ounce bottle of malt liquor (aka the 40-dog) is called milk and cookies.

Phrack Magazine

An electronic publication covering most facets of the computer underground. *Phrack* magazine has been published since 1984 and has grown to become a major source for information about operating systems, bugs, telephony, and the worldwide hacker culture.

Phreak/Phreaking

1) Originally the science and art of breaking into the phone network, usually to make free long-distance calls (phone phreak).

2) Now it also applies to breaking security barriers in any other electronic context, most often in communication networks.

Plats

Platform shoes. Though mentioned in the **Grunge Hoax,** they are authentic (see **Grunge Hoax**).

Played

1) Term describing a party or event that has peaked and has now become boring.

2) To be used, treated badly by another, stood up, or used for another's own selfish purpose. For example, "He played me."

Player

A ladies' man, drug runner, or gambler. Based on an inner-city term for a pimp.

Plug

Term for either a temp worker or a new addition to a work staff who covers work overflow. "He's a plug for Trina until she gets back in June."

FILE   EDIT   DELETE   HELP   Self-Destruct X

THE POST-NUCLEAR FAMILY

When the original Boomers were kids in the 1950s, it seemed all America was one big happy family—the nuclear family. One look at the TV shows of the period will tell you what that was like. Mom was a happy homemaker, the kids were cute, smart but generally good, and Dad—well, "Father Knew Best," right? But it wasn't long before this cozy wish-fulfillment fantasy exploded, just as Generation X was making its debut in the world; and the reality we grew up in was no sitcom.

Face it. Our generation has more experience with broken homes than any that came before us. Our parents couldn't live up to the phony ideals of *I Love Lucy* and *Leave It to Beaver,* so their marriages fractured, leaving us to pick up the pieces and invent new ways of building families.

In the '60s, while we were kids coping with divorce, TV started creating strange programs that dealt with the problem—without dealing with the problem. *The Brady Bunch* was a case in point: a widow and a widower, each with three kids, got married, with zany results. It seemed that Hollywood felt more comfortable killing off the original spouses than it did with mentioning the far more common reality of divorce. *Bewitched* exaggerated the Boomer male's paranoid fantasies about marriage by marrying him into a family of witches, while *I Dream of Jeannie* took the opposite extreme and saddled its hero with a submissive harem girl in a magic bottle.

No wonder we grew up weird. Between our own realities and the bizarre domestic lives we watched on the tube, it was inevitable that we would never be able to buy into the myth of the nuclear family.

(continued on p. 131)

Pod to Post-Nuclear Family

Pod
To faint.

Poetry Slam
A coffeehouse contest where members of the audience come on stage to read, competing for the most accolades. It can have a gong-show atmosphere, especially when accompanied by improvisational music.

Politically Retrograde
Goes back to the '50s style of politics where issues were black and white with definite left- and right-wing beliefs. Gray was not tolerated.

Pond Scum
An insult for one who is extremely low and contemptuous. Tweakers are pond scum (see **Tweeker/Tweaker**).

Pop Tarts
Cute women in post-punk pop music who cover up what they lack in intellect with pure sass.

Poppy (Music)
Radio-friendly pop with a Beatles-esque melody, but with an edge; a formula, a marketable concept, and a cute band name.

Poseur/Poser
A person pretending to be more **alternative** than he or she actually is.

Post-Ambient Sound
Aural environments that immerse the listener in their spacey and enveloping allure. While rock 'n' roll stimulates the spirit, post-ambient is lushly layered and designer-shaped to put you into a specific mental place.

Post-Boomers
People born after 1960.

Post-Nuclear Family
The family organizational unit that has become predominant, starting with the childhood of Generation X. Mom and Dad don't live together forever anymore. Now it's Mom, Uncle Joe, Mom's boyfriend, and

(continued)

THE POST-NUCLEAR FAMILY
(continued from p. 129)

(continued from p. 129)

Instead, we embrace diversity. Single mothers—and even single fathers—raise kids on their own. Gay and lesbian couples adopt children, or use surrogates or artificial insemination to actually have their own. Kids sue their parents for divorce, and get it. The post-nuclear family cannot be defined the way the nuclear family was, but we don't see that as negative at all. By trading an outworn myth for a healthy dose of truth and reality, we're more likely to raise children who can see the world clearly, instead of through the cloudy, deluded dreams of the past.

MORE:
Nuclear Waste
Nuclear Reactors
Nuclear Terrorists
Nuclear Bombs
BUT FEWER:
Nuclear Families

The Boomer television program, *My Three Sons* would change to *My Three Dads* for Generation X.

Post Nuclear Family: "Is it healthy to have eight sets of grandparents?"

"Ronald Reagan was around longer than some of my friends' fathers."

"My family is not extended. It has been junked for parts. Everyone's been divorced and remarried. Everyone's part of some other family now."

sis, Dad, Aunt June, Dad's girlfriend, etc. (see **Brady Bunch, Nuclear Family** and p. 129).

Post-Punk Power Pop

Same as poppy (see **Poppy [Music]**) but with more guitar. Format is similarly verse–chorus–verse, but with a noisy intro or bridge.

Postal

A crazy, killer, vengeance mode. "She went postal," as in a post office employee who goes crazy at work.

Posties

1) Post-Boomers.

2) People born late in the Boomer cycle who don't wish to be counted among its spawn.

Postliterate

Not able to read anything longer than a sound byte; understanding only facts, not ideas.

Postmodern

Death of the grand narrative, with its beginning, middle, and end. Left without consensus on what comprises good taste or appropriate form, we accept the equivalence of a multiplicity of styles. Las Vegas kitsch competes on the same plane as Wordsworth and a carnival freak show. Postmodern celebrates the fragment: tattoos, film clips, sound bytes, bitstream, and graffiti tags compete with the complete narrative. We freely catapult ourselves into that chaotic sea of information and images.

Post-Nirvana World

A whole rock domain up for grabs by bands that are restrained from looking too eager to assume the crown because of the non-material, non-power-tripping mindset of the alternative lifestyle.

Post-Yup

Describing the work of the affluent after the 1987 stock market tumble. It has been described as a less ostentatious world, in which making a living has replaced making a killing.

Posy-Sniffers

Derogatory term for pseudo-environmentalists, commonly shortened to sniffers. Those who champion trivial causes only to appear cool.

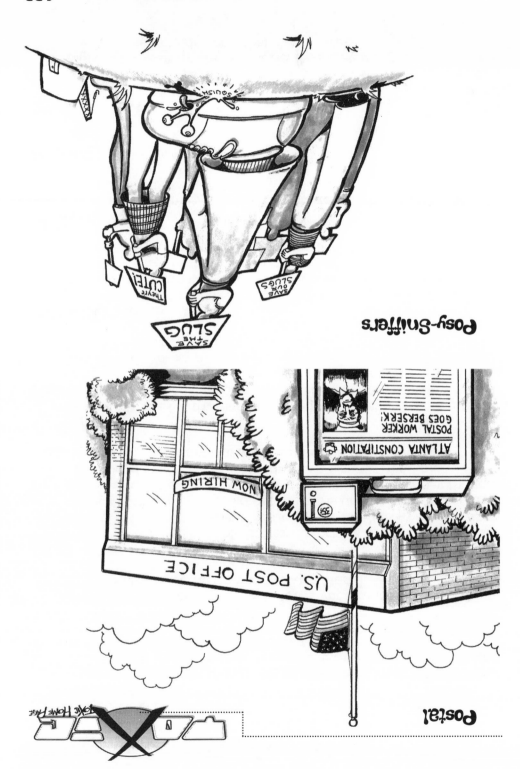

Posy-Sniffers

Postal

Poverty Jet Set to Psychographic

Poverty Jet Set

A group of people given to chronic traveling at the expense of long-term job stability or a permanent residence. They tend to have doomed and extremely expensive phone-call relationships and tend to discuss frequent-flyer programs at parties.

Progressive House Music

A mix of techno and house, with fewer vocals and a more soothing, slower rhythm (see **Techno** and **House Music**).

Prog-Rock

A somewhat dated style of progressive rock—a mix of classical music, rock 'n' roll, and psychedelia. Started in the late '60s as art rock, then classical rock. Critics who did not grasp the underlying classical structure swung the cudgel "pretentious" at the music until they thought it was dead. Procol Harum, Moody Blues, Genesis, Yes, Emerson Lake and Palmer, King Crimson, and Rush helped define the sound.

Protopunk

Early punk. The Northwest's Sonics begat The Detroit scene's Stooges and MC5, who begat the New York scene that starred Television, Patti Smith, Richard Hell, and, eventually, the Ramones, who begat the Southern California punk of Black Flag and SST Records. And that begat the explosion all over the world.

Protos/Protoadults

Kids who are too serious about life, who might as well be grown up by the time they're twelve. Frequently bent on a computer or technical career, they spurn the usual trappings of childhood and strive to assume adult form before they are emotionally mature.

Protoslackers

Those who, at times, take on the chracteristics of slackers: part-time or would-be slackers, if they only could.

Psycho Hose Beast

Nymphomaniac.

Psychographic

Marked by intense visual input. A great video game with awesome graphics could be psychographic; so could the visuals at a rave, or a highly intense sci-fi or horror movie. (Not related to the psychological use of the term to describe character profiles.)

Latchkeys

Psychotic
Really great; mega good.

Punk (Music)
Stridently angry, anti-commercial, and nihilistic rock in which energy, appearance, and attitude count for far more that talent. The Sex Pistols and the Talking Heads are two good examples.

Punk Poppers
Punk-rock bands that make it into mainstream with a three-chord sound, hook-laden lyrics (see **Hook**), and hint of melody. Bands like Green Day, Offspring, and Veruca Salt with a poppy-edged (see **Poppy [Music]**) sound, but with lyrics that are strictly punk. Punk poppers do a lot of posing and mugging and say lots of hip, irreverent things to *Rolling Stone* and *Spin* magazines.

Punkadelic Blond Dreads
Fake dreadlocks favored by skaters and the like. White boy gone rasta. See Vanilla Ice's makeover for a prime example.

Queeve
To run out of energy (in the parlance of skateboarding).

Quimby
Jerk; selfish, tactless person.

Radio-Friendly Music
The accommodation much music makes to Corporate America. A radio-friendly song needs a chorus, a catchy, hook lyric (see **Hook**), a play time of 3.2 minutes, and it needs to be non-threatening, something one can clean the house to.

Rager
An out-of-control party. A party of epic proportions.

Rainbow Gathering
First held in Colorado in the late '60s, this communal event attracts hippies, aged hobos, and contemporary counterculture denizens. Every summer, participants gather in remote woods for free camping, free food, drugs, and talk of sex. They strive for anonymity, eschewing the cash economy and corporate sponsorship. Each year the site shifts and is spread largely by word of mouth. A moving target is hard to hit.

Rager

Ranker/Rank Out

One who backs out/to back out.

Rant

One-sided oral and/or literary form of expression, as in the spoken-word performances of former Black Flag vocalist Henry Rollins. From the outside, it might appear to be ranting as the word is used in the more ordinary sense, but it is a form of discourse that involves both creativity and a consistent argument.

Rap

As a mainstream phenomenon, rap can be traced to 1984 and Run D.M.C., although it had been taking shape in the hip-hop culture nearly as long as punk. Rap is lyrical rhythmic chant, backed by sampled breaks and syncopated beats (see **Sample**). Rap is as fragmented as rock today—East Coast rappers, West Coast, gangsta rap, new school, pop rap, feminist rap (Queen Latifah), alternative **hip-hop** (Arrested Development). Today, rap is popping up in other genres—mixing with **heavy metal,** rock, reggae, jazz, **alternative,** and even country (see p. 143).

Rasta Hat

Large, colored, woven yarn hats usually worn by those with dreadlocks. Often made in yellow, green, black, and red or in other combinations. The oversized cap holds in the large dreadlocked hair of the wearer.

Rasterburn

Bloodshot eyes from extended time in front of a computer monitor.

Rasturbation

Rendering really cool things with a graphics program for entertainment value alone.

Rave

Huge, nomadic dance party that tends to last all night, or until the police show up, usually with **techno** music and psychedelic mood enhancers. There may be a light show, and dress is usually retro (see **Retro**). Raves are usually located at different and illegal places, such as warehouses, and are not advertised by traditional means, but by flyers and word of mouth. Directions are both secretive and cryptic to avoid authorities (see p. 141).

Rave

Rave Boys

Young men who fashion themselves after medieval court jesters and go to all-night, drug-addled raves. It's been said that many jesters of the Middle Ages had some sort of retardation or brain damage, which these current **posers** can only hope to have.

Raver

Someone who attends **raves** and adopts (at least for that evening) the cultural trappings of the rave phenomenon.

Rave-Scene Art

Art that concentrates on eye games (like 3-D stereograms), and psychedelia; can be made via computer.

Rave Techno

As with any new music form, the record companies eventually get wise to what's going on in the real world and try to cash in. While there are some good artists working in this more commercial area, the general sound is less aggressive, is more likely to feature vocals, and is frequently **rap**- or reggae-influenced.

Raw

Great; very good; good-looking.

Razor Boy/Girl

A cybernetically augmented thug in the fictional world of cyberpunk.

Real Slice, A

A bad day.

Rebelaisian

Referring to a rebel without a clue.

Regression Hangouts

Return-to-the-womb nightclubs and coffee shops. They are decorated like nurseries or romper rooms. Next to these regression hangouts are retro-toy shops and retro-boutiques that sell favorite old toys and vintage clothing (see also **Retro-banks**).

Ren and Stimpy

Ren Hoek, a hyperneurotic cartoon chihuahua, and Stimpson J. Cat, his cheerfully dopey sidekick, became Generation X icons when their crude-humored but surrealistic cartoon show appeared on the

(continued)

RAVES

A rave is an underground party that is usually thrown by a group of young adults and can range from several hundred people dancing to a portable sound system in an open field, to thousands of people gathered for an immense party in a warehouse or outdoor location. Larger raves can feature many different areas where people can dance to different kinds of music. Many raves, especially the bigger ones, are put on by promoters with the sole purpose of making money.

The smaller, truly underground raves are the most interesting and often the most fun. Most of these rarely take place at the same place twice, since they are considered illegal gatherings by the police. It's easier and cheaper to set up a secret location than it is to pay for permits, and besides, going to an illegal party is more thrilling. Larger raves pose a different problem: it's hard to get thousands of people together without anybody noticing. Rave organizers get around this by having their events on private property, or on Indian reservations, where state and local authorities can't stop them. If a rave is broken up by the police, the organizers usually honor the tickets for that rave at the next one they put on.

Rave organizers often spare no expense to create colorful, psychedelic flyers that double as "works of art"and give the party-goer the location, date, and DJ line-up. While flyers are available free at clubs, record shops, clothing stores, and other locations, they frequently become collectors' items. Flyers from the early days of the rave scene are jealously hoarded by fanatical collectors, so be sure to hang onto any that come your way.

In order to keep the cops away, rave organizers usually don't announce their location until the night of the event. Generally,

(continued on p. 145)

Nickelodeon cable network. After two seasons, the network booted series creator John Kricfalusi; what remained was still obsessed with bodily fluids and other anatomical by-products, but the transcendent madness of the original vision was lost.

Repair Generation

Referring to post-Boomer generations who will try to repair the mess left by the **Boomer** and Silent generations.

Retro-

Another prefix that can be added to any word to indicate a hip or hyped return to the past.

Retro-Banks

Well-stocked vintage clothing stores for buying, selling, and trading.

Ricky Racer

Mountain-bike racer wannabe. He has all the accessories, cruises the boardwalk and bike trails, but only occasionally races, if at all.

Rider

Very negative term for someone who tags along when unwanted; a copy cat.

Ridic

Ridiculous.

Robo Babe

Term used to describe a beautiful woman that the describer will never have. For the Robo Babe, brains are optional; she knows it and not much else.

Robo Squid

Military-looking police with white helmets, mirror glasses, and black, leather-clad uniforms. See the bad guy in the movie *Terminator II* with "Arnie" Schwarzenegger (see **Squid**).

Robidosing

Another quasi-legal high, favored by adolescents. Involves chugging over-the-counter cough syrups like Robitussin (hence the name). If Mom and Dad's chock-full-of-codeine prescription syrups are available, even better.

Repair Generation

RAP

The Guiness Book of World Records has recognized Daddy Freddy as the world's fastest rapper. Speech pathologist Dr. John Haskkell confirmed that Daddy can utter 528 syllables per minute. (*Spin* Magazine)

"In its constantly changing slang and shifting concerns—no other pop has so many antidrug songs—rap's flood of words presents a fictionalized oral history of a brutalized generation." (Jon Pareles, *New York Times*)

Rock

1) A basketball. "Pass me the rock."

2) Crack cocaine. Both terms seem to have originated in the inner city.

Rock-On

A happy good-bye. "Rock on, dude!" Though mentioned in the Grunge Hoax (see **Grunge Hoax**), it was authentic.

Roids

Steroids.

Roll Out

To leave. "These guys lag, let's roll out."

Rouge

To steal.

Sagger

Old Man.

Salsa Romantica

Spanish love songs with sumptuous Caribbean rhythm arrangements that have carried singers like Mexico's Luis Miguel into the Top 30 of *Billboard's* pop album chart.

Sampling

A staple of modern music, sampling digitizes sounds that can be played back in a variety of forms. Some performers have used this technology to interesting effect: Graeme Revell's obscure album *The Insect Musicians* created an orchestra with sounds sampled from nearly eighty different species of insects. But **rap,** and later **techno,** used sampling to "quote" from older music, a practice that, at its worst, involved lifting basslines and drum beats wholesale. At its best, it can be used as a commentary on modern culture (as practiced by the group Negativland), or to create a unique sonic palette that doesn't refer to other people's work at all.

Sans

French word meaning "without." Caffeine sans LaCreme. Auteur sans direction. Rebel sans clue.

RAVES *(continued from p. 141)*

a recorded message will inform callers where to find a checkpoint where they can buy their tickets and get maps to the rave. Sometimes the first checkpoint will only tell you where to find the next checkpoint. And so on . . . and so on . . .

DJs are an essential part of the rave scene. People will come from other states to hear top DJs spin live—each one has their own distinct style. **Techno** and **House Music** are popular for the heavy dance workout while **Ambient** rooms provide a respite from the thundering beats with a more relaxing music.

Expect everything and anything to happen. Sometimes a rave is just like a regular club, where everybody dances and has a good time. Larger raves can be massive events that feel like a carnival, where different areas feature a variety of DJs each playing their own blend of music. They can feature entertainers, acrobats, dancers, firebreathers, live musicians like Crash Worship, and booths where you can get your body pierced, buy clothing made of hemp, and get food and drink. Alcohol, however, isn't real popular with the rave crowd. Drugs like Ecstasy and pot are more common. But it is the people you'll meet there who are really the most important part of any rave.

While there are still plenty of people who dress up for raves in platform shoes and big Dr. Seuss hats, there are just as many people from all walks of life who go to them as well. Don't be surprised to see a handful of older people there among the youthful crowd. A lot of people from the '60s see raves as a natural outgrowth of the love-ins they went to in their own younger days. There have been raves that were disrupted by violent behavior, but these are the exception; most people at raves are just there to have a good time (see flyer on p. 147).

Santeria Music

Music inspired by or related to the rituals of the Santeria religion, a Caribbean mixture of African and Catholic traditions similar in some ways to voudon (voodoo). Driving, hypnotic music with a definite Afro/Caribbean feel.

Sappnin'

What's happening?

Sappy

Goofy, dopey, yet somewhat classic.

Scam

To pick up women or men for purposes of sexual entertainment.

Scarification

People bored with tattoos are turning in greater numbers to scarification, the burning of designs directly into their flesh. Tattoos can be removed; with scarification, you're commited for life (see p. 173).

Scarlet Braces

The red suspender favored by old-school skinheads, indicating "We've just got violence on our minds."

Scenic

An event or occurrence that causes unwanted attention. "Then Mona started screaming at the waiter for dropping her cheese sticks on the floor. It was so scenic."

Schwag

Poor-grade Mexican **buds;** dope; marijuana.

Scoop

To kiss someone.

Score

1) To acquire or get. "I gotta score the new Slim Whitman album, he **shreds** hard."

2) An exclamation meaning "great." "They gave us four extra tacos in the drive-thru and didn't charge us. . . . SCORE!" Definition 2 derives from the infamous Grunge Hoax, but has fallen into actual use (see **Grunge Hoax**).

FEATURING:
D.J. TOXIC
AND
THE HEAVY METAL SOUNDS OF
MELTDOWN
TOXIE
TIME: 10:00 TILL ?
PLACE:
RAVE WAREHOUSE
BILLBOARD ST.
S. DIEGO
TOXIE
RAVE
ALL U NEED IS
10 OF DEEZ

Scrappin'

Fighting.

Scrut

To eat voraciously.

Server

A computer that holds information that can be accessed by other computers.

Shareware

Computer software that is distributed at no cost with the understanding that if the user finds it of value they will pay a fee to the originator of the program.

SHARPs

SkinHeads Against Racial Prejudice. A splinter group of young **skinheads** who want to enjoy the lifestyle, but without the stigma of being ignorant and abusive. They distance themselves from the ideas, but not the dress and music.

Shred

To surf, snowboard, or skate extremely well.

Shrooms

Mushrooms containing the hallucinogenic drug psilocybin.

Sick

Cool, phat, great. "Dude, that's really sick. I love it."

Silverfoxes

Retirees who, as young eyes see it, are awash in money and wealth, live in nice houses, and drive expensive motorhomes.

S/TCOMs

Single Income, Two Children, Oppressive Mortgage. What yuppies turn into when they have children and one stops working to be with the kids. The true martyrs of Reaganomics, as characterized in *The Economist*.

Sixer

Six-pack of beer.

SHARPs

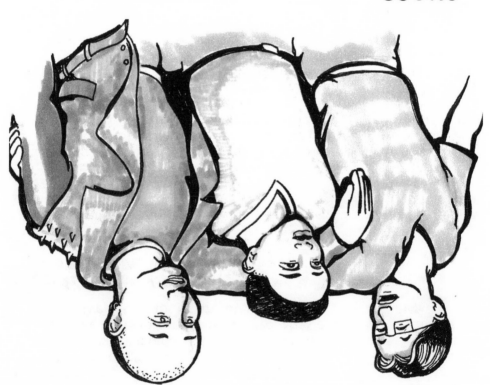

Ska

Dance music popular in Jamaica in the '60s mainly through the Skatalites and Toots & the Maytals. Ska is characterized by heavy use of brass, especially the saxophone, with a heavily accented offbeat. Ska shows influences of rhythm and blues and jazz. The sound has enjoyed a revival since the early '80s through British groups like English Beat. Today Pennywise and the Mighty Mighty Bosstones carry on the ska tradition, folded into a punk sensibility.

Skeezer

The type of girl your grandfather may have called a punch board. A skeezer is not a prom date or a "lunch with mom" date. She's an easy time in the bathroom of some dive. She's a woman who makes sex feel alive, if only for ten minutes.

Sketch/Sketchy/Sketcher

To **flake** out/an undesirable scenario/one who's on drugs.

Skiffle

Pre-Beatles British folk-pop, usually played on street corners for change.

Skinheads

Young thugs who subscribe to a fascist belief structure. The skinheads originated in England in the middle of the twentieth century as a response to the influx of immigrants. They enjoy angry music, angry books, and angry lifestyles. Racist skinheads can sometimes be spotted wearing scarlet braces, and white laces in Doc Marten boots are topped off with at least one tattoo proclaiming their beliefs (See also **SHARPs (Skinheads Against Racial Prejudice** [p. 149]), **Scarlet Braces,** and **Doc Martens).**

Skree

Loose rock and gravel that shreds skin when a biker falls off of his mountain bike on a killer downhill run.

Slacker

A rebel against the Puritan work ethic. A generic term for one who does not attempt to live up to society's expectations and who is usually perceived as a burden. Slacker implies laziness and a lack of motivation and direction toward any perceivable goal other than to enjoy oneself. Today's era of instant millionaires, mega-dollar sales prices for

(continued)

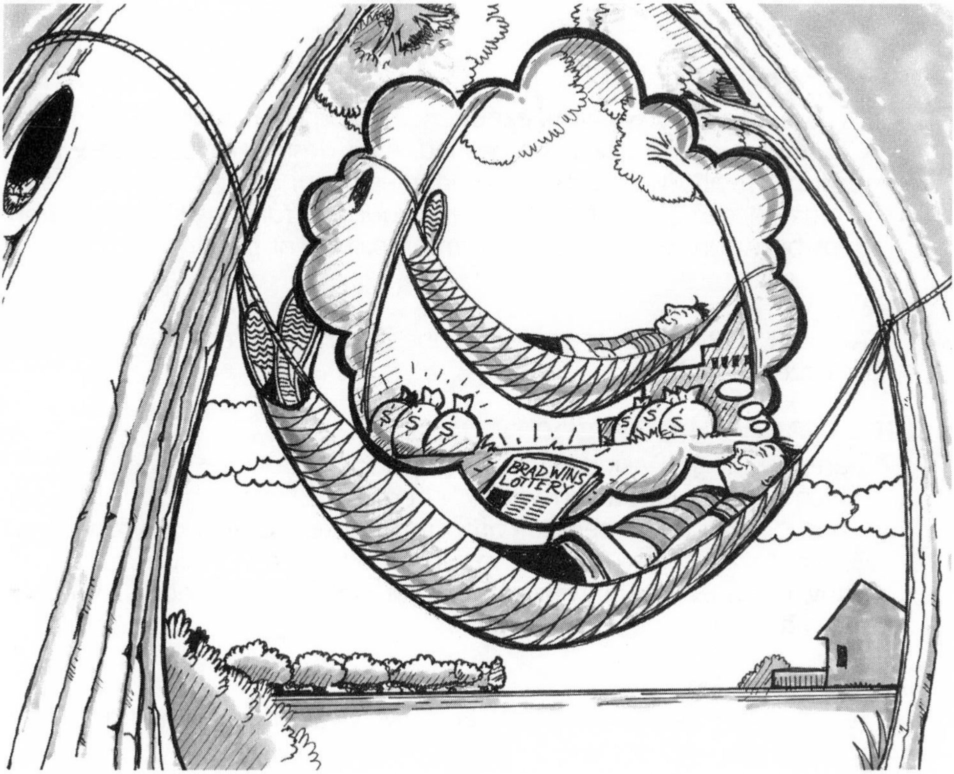

Slacker

Slacker stealing from work = an action of economic protest

Slacker guerilla tactic = sleeping in

Slacker = Millennial guerilla in an extreme energy-saving mode

---

SKINHEADS

"We've just got violence on our minds."

---

contemporary products, and ideas that can be merched (see **Merched**), in contrast to the proliferation of low-paying, service-sector jobs, feeds this slacker idea of laying back to think and relax and wait for "it" to happen to them.

Slacker Resume

A résumé that shows work experience doing creative things at places where employment can't be verified, e.g., designer, illustrator, writer, or public-relations person for companies no longer in business. It also avoids showing the frequent unaccounted for, missing-in-inaction gaps between relatively short-term employment positions.

Slag

To insult, to criticize, to put someone down. "I hate to slag him, but he's such a fool."

Slam Dance/Slamming

Started with Sid Vicious doing the pogo at early Sex Pistols shows, which begat slam dancing, which begat moshing, which begat jock types looking to hit people without the threat of real confrontation. Originally an outlet for outcasts to take their aggression out harmlessly, it has evolved into an excuse for violence. And now, someone often gets hurt.

Slasher Movie

As defined by film critic Roger Ebert, "Movies starring a mad-dog killer who runs amok, slashing all of the other characters."

Sled

A large '70s-era vehicle that is cheap, large, comfy transportation, and disposable. It is also recyclable (see **Hooptie**).

Sludge

The bottom of the coffee pot after it has cooked all day. Many X'ers work two jobs and this is the result of their morning job and what greets them at their evening job. Sludge contains at least eight times the caffeine of regular coffee. What it gains in stimulants, it sorely lacks in taste.

Sludge-o-Mania

Manic state created by ingesting large amounts of caffeine.

THE SLACKER RÉSUMÉ:
PERSONAL SPIN CONTROL

How does a slacker use a résumé to get a real, paying job? By creatively reinventing the past through personal spin control.

December 1991 to March 1992: Part-time freelance beta tester for Nintendo, Sega, and other gaming software companies. Translation: Spent most of free time hanging out in arcades and at friends' houses playing video games.

April 1992 to September 1992: Assistant public-relations supervisor at a major theme park. Translation: Wore a walrus suit and greeted visitors at Sea World until the summer season ended.

October 1992 to December 1992: Educational sabbatical. Translation: Slept.

January 1993 to August 1993: Telecommunications specialist, with emphasis on maintenance of telephone systems. Translation: Worked in a series of telemarketing jobs selling scam coupon books; location changed every few months as employers tried to avoid the fraud squad.

September 1993 to November 1993: Volunteer work as a live-in companion to invalid adult as part of annual charity work. Translation: Lived at mom's house for three months until fed up with mowing the lawn, washing dishes, and surveillance.

December 1993 to March 1994: Extensive technical training in software analysis. Translation: Couch-surfed at various friends' houses and played video games up to eighteen hours a day.

April 1994 to June 1994: Full-time beta tester for major game companies. Translation: Got really good at video games, gave up sleeping.

July 1994 to January 1996: Program analyst for major software company. Translation: Actually got a job as a beta tester for a major game company. Still played games all week but finally got paid for it.

February 1996 to date: Pursuing a career in the culinary arts, with special emphasis on becoming a professional *saucier.* Translation: Flip burgers at McDonald's and unload weekly shipments of Special Sauce.

Slurpage
Any kind of drink, but usually alcohol.

Smack Addled
Strung out on heroin. Not uncommon among all generations. A number of Gen X heroes have been addicts: William S. Burroughs, Jim Carroll, and Kurt Cobain, to name a few. Though it sounds happy-go-lucky, it definitely has a grim meaning. Slang is one method of masking and lightening reality and this term is evidence of that.

Smart Bar
Establishment that serves "cocktails" containing cognitive-enhancement drugs, frequently served at raves (see **Rave**).

Smiley
The most widely used emoticon (a means of communicating emotion through text characters). Smiley looks like this :-) and is somewhat akin to the happy face of the '70s.

Smoke a Bowl
In other words, relax. A way of telling someone to calm down; also an offer to smoke pot.

Smurfing
Money-laundering procedure by which currency is exchanged at various banks in amounts slightly less than what must be reported to federal authorities. These amounts change, but when all transactions of $10,000 or more had to be reported, many transactions took place involving $9,999. In these times of increasing scrutiny, the "safe" amount is constantly being lowered.

Snake
To steal.

Snap
1) To criticize, harass.
2) Trading snaps, or snapping, is a venerable tradition of swapping inventive insults, often regarding your opponent's mother. Wit and one-upmanship are the key to success in this competition.
3) To break a promise. A snapper can be one who breaks a promise.

Smart Bar

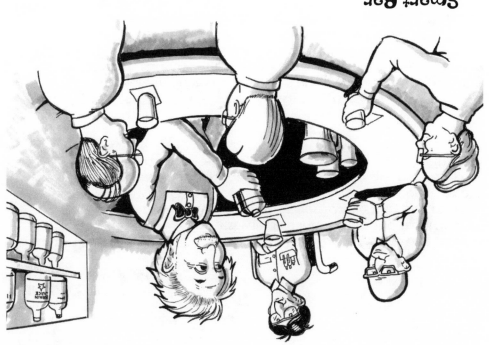

Snap Back
Fight back against being bullied or picked on.

Snapped On
Picked on, bullied.

Snaps
1) Money.

2) Credit, praise. "You should get snaps for that."

Sniff
Cocaine.

Souped
To be conceited.

South by Southwest Music Convention (SXSW)
Annual **alternative** music festival, held in the bars and nightclubs of Austin, Texas, previewing the best unsigned talent in the country. With each new "discovery" comes a rising deluge of corporate record label A&R geeks and rock critics. Bands really do get discovered at SXSW, as they do at the CMJ Alternative Music Conference in New York City.

Spam
1) Posting of a single message across many different Internet newsgroups. More frequently, businesses are spamming ads across the **Internet.** Net users often respond in kind, spamming the originator of an annoying message until the source's computer is overloaded. The source of the word is believed to be Monty Python's hilarious short-order restaurant sketch in which everything is made with spam.

2) A term meaning cool or great.

Spammin'
1) Speaking aimlessly on a variety of subjects.

2) Attempting to stuff someone's brain with information of questionable truth or value. "This dweeb started spammin' me about how Madonna and Michael Jackson are funding a secret political organization."

ENTREPRENEURS

There is a wave sweeping the nation amongst twentysomethings and we ain't talking that thing people do with their hands at monstrous sporting events. It's called entrepreneurship and what it means is that many of the very same youths you deemed slackers and lazy no-gooders have taken the flailing economy into their own hands and started their very own companies.

It's the D.I.Y. attitude's emergence into adulthood. (D.I.Y. is an aesthetic that translates to "Do It Yourself,"a catch phrase from punk rock wherein the musicians weren't looking for a hand-up from the major record label but rather, formed their own small garage record labels at home.) And now is the dawn of D.I.Y. carried to the corporate level.

Couple this idealistic yet realistic passion to take control of their own lives with the computer literacy that todays' youth's inheritantly possess and bingo! You got yourself a multinational.

The generation you call X is the most likely to start their own business, more likely than their **Boomer** parents or even their grandparents, according to a Roper Starch Survey from 1993. Another study conducted at Marquette University estimates that 7 million U.S. adults are currently attempting to start up a new business. That study also claims that nearly eight in ten of those Americans applying for loans, drawing up business plans and renting space, are between the ages of 18 and 34.

As magazines deem the generation grungy and dirty, lazy and apathetic, many of those very youths, who may very well be dirty and most certainly are apathetic, are proving

(continued on p. 163)

Spaz

To lose control of one's emotions.

Spazzing

Making a big deal about something.

Spew

1) To get rid of.

2) To vomit.

Spin Control/Spin Doctors

Creating and managing the story that you want the public to believe. Spin Doctors or Spin Controllers tied up any loose ends of Reagan's "great communicating" and made sure all damage was contained. Spin control is a manipulator's tool. It is also known as fleshing out, reinterpreting, or embellishing. In other words, lying.

Spliff

A large marijuana cigarette.

Spokesdude/Spokesmanic

Spokesperson, MC, etc. The Dan Cortese guy on MTV. The ladies think he's hot, and the guys think he's cool. Fonzie with a teleprompter.

Sponsorship

To have someone purchase cocktails for you with no strings attached. A cynical play on Alcoholics Anonymous's "sponsor."

Spot

1) On the mark in a highly positive fashion, as in "Spot on!"

2) To front (loan) somebody something: "Can you spot me a twenty for tickets?"

Square

Cigarette.

Spun

Crazy, addled. "That chick is so spun. She really believes she's Uma Thurman."

Squid

Military-looking nerd (see **Robo Squid**).

"We're definitely going to need the spin doctors on this one!"

Squid Lips

Fool or moron.

Stack

To make a lot of money.

Stage Diving

When performers (sometimes fans) jump off the stage into the mosh pit crowd at a concert (see **Mosh Pit**).

Stankey

Olfactorally offensive; stinks! A very bad smell, rancid.

Sexually Transmitted Diseases. As in "Gonasyphaherpalaids (gonorrhea–syphilis–herpes–AIDS)."

Stems

Legs. "He's got great stems." Á la 1940s.

Stoner

Someone who smokes marijuana as a vocation.

Strangelove Ocean

1) From the movie *Doctor Strangelove*. Ecology slang for an ocean where pollution has killed all the life forms near the water's surface, making it look like a nuked wasteland.

2) Any ecologically devastated area (see **Eco-Villain**).

Strapped

Carrying a gun.

Stupid Fresh

Outstanding or spectacular; more than plain fresh in **rap** terminology (see **Fresh**).

Stud-Muffin

An immodest, good-looking guy.

Sub Pop

In 1988, a fledgling Seattle record label called Sub Pop released a three-CD box set called Sub Pop 200. A compilation of bands like Nirvana, Soundgarden, and Mudhoney, it came complete with a 20-page booklet packed with pictures by Charles Peterson, the photo–

(continued)

FILE   EDIT   DELETE   HELP   Self-Destruct X

STDs: SEXUALLY TRANSMITTED DISEASES
GONASYPHAHERPALAIDS

In the age when STDs can kill you slowly or quickly, but still very dead, deader than a Bible Belt Preacher in Iran, sex without condoms is much like playing Russian roulette with two bullets instead of one.

CONDOM SEX

Another gift to future generations. However, great forward thrusts have been made in the design and development of these **jimmy caps.** Multi colors, flavors, textures, and even cartoons adorn these latex dikes that hold back the disease-laden seas of sex.

"I feel stupid and contagious."
(Nirvana, "Smells Like Teen Spirit")

grapher credited with creating grunge's hair-sweat-and-guitars look. Sub Pop also sent a catalogue to the nation's alternative-rock intelligentsia describing its band's punk-metal guitar noise as "grunge." Troubled by cash-flow problems, the company's biggest success came when they sold Nirvana's contract to Geffen Records for over $70,000 and a percentage of the profits on the band's first Geffen release.

S'up

Contraction for "What's up?"

Sunflower

Cute girl.

Sweat

1) To trash; to break something.

2) To give someone a bad time.

Sweater Puppies

Breasts.

Sweet

Cool; good.

Swing Kids

New movement of hipsters who borrow from the culture of the '40s, as opposed to the current trend of borrowing from the '60s and '70s.

Swordfight

A party or gathering where the male-to-female ratio is lopsided. The place to be if you are on the outnumbered side.

Sybarite

A sensualist. One who believes in pleasure first; a distinct hedonist but with a tribal bent.

Synthespian

Synthetic actor. Used in 3-D computer-animation lingo to describe sophisticated human forms that can be imported into a virtual world. Also called electronic puppets, dolls, or vactors.

System

Stereo system, sound system.

ENTREPRENEURS *(continued from p. 157)*

they ain't so much lazy. It's been seared into the skulls of this generation that the American Dream is not accessible via the same paths their parents paved. So, in response, many are finding their own way to get it. Apathetic maybe, but lazy, not on your life. One of the things the above-mentioned studies proved was that the twentysomethings were working day jobs to finance their creative American Dreams, and finding, more often than not, that eventually that double duty paid off.

What so much of the media seems to forget in their assessment of Gen X is that this is the generation raised with computers in their schools and homes. Twentysomethings have never been scared of the computer because, for them, it has never been an unknown. They are the first generation with this power and, even though they may not be running in droves to Brooks Brothers for those power suits and hitting the chi-chi-est haunts for their power lunches, there are still many walking and talking the power. They're just working too hard to flaunt it.

And the youthful apathy toward all things big and governmental still persists. Another study conducted in 1994 for the youth political advocacy group Third Millennium revealed that more twentysomethings believed in UFOs than the idea that Social Security money will be intact when they retire. That's right, twentysomethings of today don't feel the way to secure a financially sound future is up the staid corporate ladder. They'd have a better chance winning the lottery, or perhaps being abducted by rich aliens from outerspace. Or rolling those scary dice of chance and starting their own business from the ground up.

Tadow

All right! An expression indicating something cool has been done or achieved. From "take a bow."

Talk outside One's Neck

To lie or tease.

Talk to the Seals

Surfer's term for vomiting.

Tamale Time

A time to be embarrassed for doing something stupid or uncool. "It's tamale time for that dude."

Tard

Someone who is moving or acting slowly, or apparently with sudden lack of intellect. From the word *retard*.

Taste of the Boo

Drugs, including alcohol. "Yo, G, wanna taste of the boo?"

Tattoos

The contemporary fashion statement. Personal statements placed on that ideological billboard of the '90s, the human body (see p 173).

Tchotchke

A term for stuff in general, little stuff, big stuff, whatever. In computer lingo, it can refer to all the extras you've slapped onto your computer, whether they really help it work better or not.

Techno

A stripped-down, hard-driving music, usually without vocals, that took the funk/electronic direction of house and electrofunk to a new, sped-up extreme. Originating in Detroit, techno was well established by 1985 and soon became the standard party music at raves (see **House Music, Rave,** and **Techno House Music**).

Techno Tweaking

Obsessive attention to technical detail in the use of computers and an interest in technology to the exclusion of all other concerns. A tendency of **alpha geeks.** Can also refer to a complete and mindless immersion in the heavy beats of **techno** music.

Just think of the possibilities of Olympic Game advertising where the athletes are not permitted to wear apparel displaying corporate logos during competition but no restrictions have been made on tattoos.

I can picture it now—an Olympic sportscaster says:

"Strutting into the boxing ring is Erik Bergman, with a bright red Toshiba emblazoned on his . . . um . . . upper leg. He is in tremendous shape as you can see by his muscular chest, which is large enough to display 'Cecils Refrigerator Repair Service since 1985.'"

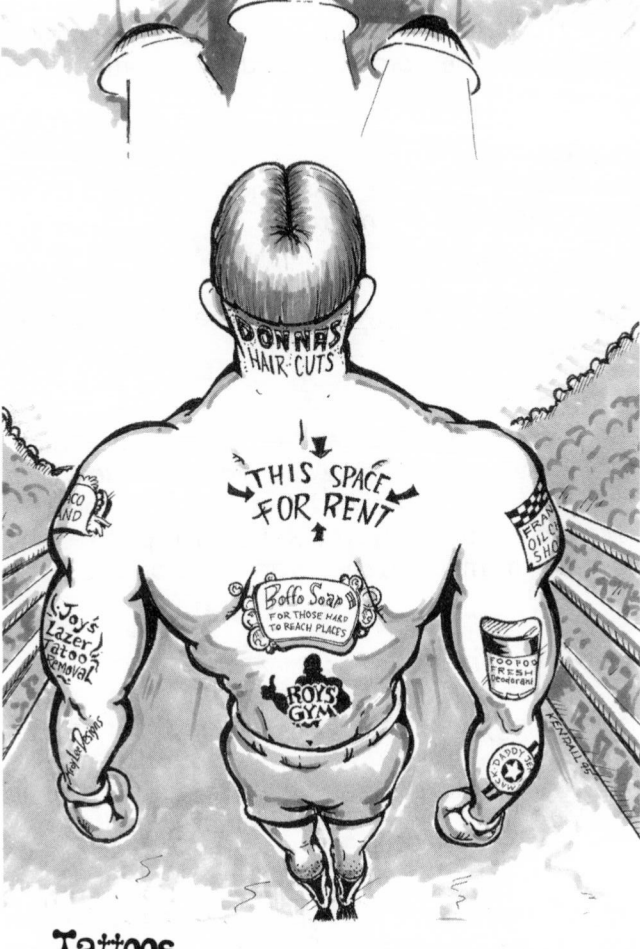

Tattoos
(See also p. 173.)

TATTOOS ARE PERSONAL STATEMENTS

"My body is the one thing that I have control over. I can use it to express what I like, what I think is important, beautiful, meaningful—what I feel."

Technobabies

The rising breed of Generation Y: little kids taught on classroom computers from an early age who know more about computers than Bill Gates by the time they're ten years old. If you think technology is accelerating now, wait until they grow up and start getting their hands on things.

Techno House Music

A combination of **techno** and **house** that tends to have a faster drumbeat, from 126 to 140 beats per minute.

Technolust

Having a gadget, gizmo, tech, or hardware fetish. Fondness for consumer electronic gadgetry.

Techno Savant Writing

Jargon-heavy descriptions of technology and/or its role in the future of human society, largely incomprehensible to ordinary people. Often found in the pages of *Wired* magazine, or, in a somewhat more psychedelic mode, in *Mondo 2000*. Often written by smart people who know a lot, but not nearly as much as they want us to believe.

Techno Shamanism

A unique end-of-the-millennium anachronism spawned by computer-intensive, drug-saturated navel gazers with a hankering for spiritual meaning. Modern technology doesn't have to drive us farther from communion with the universe, they argue: It can be used as a tool to realize ancient shamanistic practices in the here and now. Cranks to some, visionaries to others, they seek the best of both worlds.

Techno Weenie

Lost in the labyrinth of modern techno-hype. The techno weenie buys every new expensive gimmick but can't actually use it in an even remotely intelligent fashion. Techno-weenie bike lore: The guy who bought the lightest titanium bike, best and lightest components, aero wheels, aero helmet, skin suit, everything to reduce wind drag and rolling resistance, but continued to weigh 250 lbs.

Tejano

Music that combines the accordion-driven polkas and cumbias of Mexican *conjunto* music with modernizing touches, including synthesizers and versions of rock songs; it has a core audience of young Mexican Americans, reaching from the Southwest to California.

INFORMATION OVERLOAD
SOUNDBYTING: THE NEXT STEP IN EVOLUTION

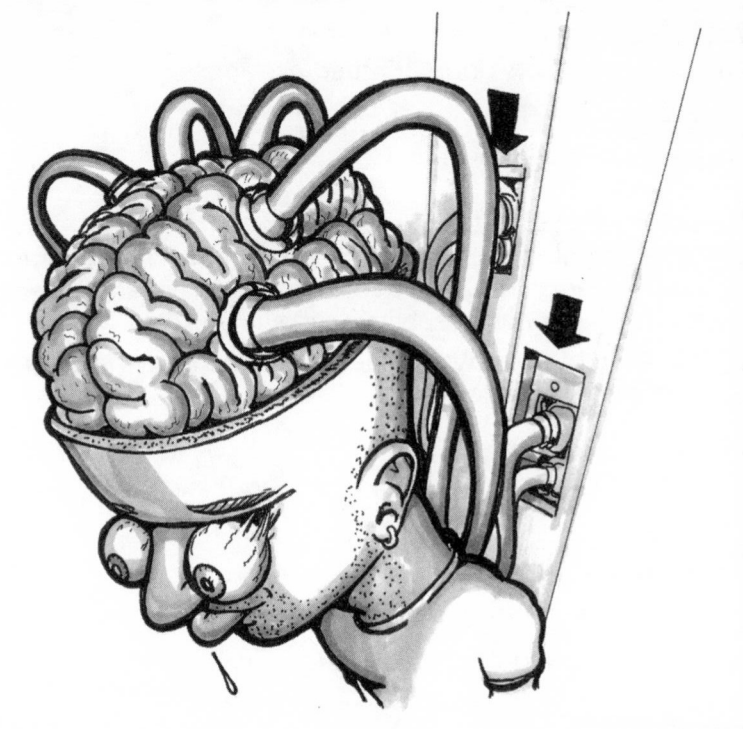

Out there on the information superhighway, the traffic is getting heavier even as the speed limit increases unimaginably. There's more information, more choices, more often—and in ever more tightly compressed time frames.

Because the brain hasn't changed much in the last 100,000 years or so, and has shown no sign of upcoming improvements, it is utterly impossible for us to process even a tiny

(continued on p. 169)

Telephone Number Salary

A seven-digit salary (or project budget). What every slacker wants (without much work), whether they admit it or not.

Tent Pole

A girl so sexy that she creates a tent pole in guys' pants. An "erectoress."

That Bites/This Bites

Awful, unpleasant, terrible, not good.

That Rules

"That's cool." "That's dope." Excited exclamation of approval.

That Rocks

"That's cool." "That's great."

Third-World Revolution

1) The electronic revolution that frees us from the geographical confines of Earth. The first two revolutions generally freed us from physical slavery and repetitive tasks.

2) The battle by Third-World countries to achieve the economic status of affluent countries.

Thirtysomethings

Those in their thirties (see p. 175).

Thrasher

1) Skateboarder.

2) Skateboarder who doesn't give a damn.

3) A magazine about skateboarding.

Thrifting

Living a lifestyle that was once based on poor personal economics that forced one to shop for and wear clothing from thrift/second-hand stores, such as Goodwill and Salvation Army. Usually lots of flannel. It has become a pseudo nonfashion statement for the thoroughly merched grunge fashion chic and is no longer a cheap way to get clothes. Even thrift stores are charging the going rate, à la Nordstroms (see **Grunge, Merch**).

Throat Yogurt

Phlegm deposits in the throat from excessive smoking.

INFORMATION OVERLOAD
(continued from p. 167)

fraction of what comes pouring off the smallest information highway offramp. Soundbyting helps users (also known as humans) deal with the flow of information by serving as both a focus and a filter.

Soundbyting is communicating and processing information in short, efficient, stand-alone units.

Unlike fleshed-out, wordy paragraphs strung together through the use of conjunctive words and phrases, soundbyting cuts right to the quick with tight wording, omitting the niceties found in leisurely worded literature.

Now, the idea of receiving and transmitting only essential data sans the literary baggage, often offends some older folks who find themselves resisting change, as they still cling to the belief that old-fashioned, word-laden communication methods are culturally superior.

Superior? Today it is, in a word, inadequate.

Not that we don't appreciate well-crafted literature. We do— in its place. But that place is becoming smaller and smaller. Where once it was a necessity, it is now a luxury. Terrific—if you can afford it.

Soundbyting data is nothing new; you're filtering information right now. Look around you. Listen, smell, feel: Is there a ticking clock you've been ignoring? Some movement off to your left that you long since figured out was cars gliding on a distant freeway, and now pay no attention? An itch that you successfully blocked out until you just went searching for it?

We're also able to handle an incredible amount of incoming data. On more conventional highways, you've undoubtedly done something like this: Involved in a mild argument with a significant other while driving, you make a pretty convincing

(continued on p. 171)

Thumb Candy

A computer game requiring eye–hand coordination and little brain power.

Tits

Something amazing, awesome. "That movie was tits!"

To Break It Down

To turn down the music.

Toxic

1) Astonishing, attention grabbing.

2) Strong, fierce.

Track

1) To talk.

2) To understand.

Tragic Cash

1) Money saved for a very rainy day.

2) Fundage acquired by a death (see **Fundage**).

Train Wreck

When two or more musicians play conflicting parts at the same time, resulting in a few seconds of musical chaos; making its way into the general vernacular as an expression for any creative catastrophe.

Trance

A very dreamy type of dance music, trance tends to be faster than ambient (see **Ambient**).

Trekkie Technobabble

The juvenile pseudotechnical language spoken by a Trekkie (as in *Star Trek*).

Tremolo Bars

A whammy bar on guitar. In the heyday of glam metal, it was used to bend strings into different ranges of feedback or to sound like a banshee being dragged across flames (see **Glam Metal**).

INFORMATION OVERLOAD
(continued from p. 169)

point even as you downshift from third to second while lining up an open slot for a left turn (there's a space right after that pick-up passes), noting at the same time that the new R.E.M. song just came on the radio, while some part of your mind calculates that if you hit the next three green lights, you'll make the movie on time if that moron ahead of you speeds up a little bit.

Pretty impressive. And somewhere around one-billionth of the info that's now available every nanosecond.

And books written for those with Attention Deficit Disorder (ADD) often use soundbyting as a tool to help readers focus on the written words while so much other stimulus attempts to grab away their attention.

Even slang is a form of soundbyting. Several words are compressed into a single word or phrase.

So in fact, we need help—we need soundbyting. At least, until a genetically engineered computer chip, implanted directly into the brain, can do some of the filtering for us. Soundbyting is not a passing cultural phenomena. It is here to stay until the next evolutionary step that may include implanting computer chips directly into the brain. In his 1984 book, *Neuromancer,* William Gibson names this brain-implanted computer chip "Microsoft." I wonder if Bill Gates has a microsoft we don't know about.

"Do sound bites swallow substance, as the critics say? Read Einstein's lips—$E=mc^2$—and a scientific revolution is born; the Ten Commandments—the Ten Sound Bites—and monotheism makes its debut. Jefferson pens "Life, Liberty, and the Pursuit of Happiness" and a sound bite is heard 'round the world."

Andrew Savitz and Mark Katz, "Sound Bites Have Teeth," in the *New York Times*

Tribal

A percussion-based style that incorporates elements such as bongos and African vocal chants. The band Exquisite Corpse is one example.

Trick Rig

A girl or guy with a great body has a trick rig.

Trife

1) Living without a basic sense of morality or purpose.

2) Unethical; lacking any morals or ecological responsibility. "The awesome trife profit-seeking intellect of Corporate Amerika."

Trip-hoppers

People into trip-hop, a music created where **hip-hop** and **rave** culture meet on the fringes of acid jazz. More low-down and funky than its close relatives, this music is closer to the street than acid jazz, and so are the people in the trip-hop scene.

Triscuit

To be a flake, an airhead. "Don't be a triscuit."

Trompe L'Oeil

That which deceives the eye.

Tropical

A catch-all term for up-tempo Caribbean music, from Cuban *rhumba* to Puerto Rican *bamba* and *plena* to Dominican *merengue* and all their hybrids. Performers like Juan Luis Guerra, a Dominican song-writer who has dabbled in styles from Dominican *bachatas* (ballads) to West African *soukous,* have audiences that span the hemisphere.

'Tude

An attitude, usually a bad and misplaced one.

Tweak

Term for crystal methamphetamine.

Tweaked

1) Broken, as in played too loud or stretched too far.

2) Manipulated, twisted, and turned into something different. This could be a machine, an instrument, a guitar, a character in a book or play, or a person under pressure.

3) To be spun on crystal methamphetamine.

TATTOOING, BRANDING, AND SCARIFICATION

There was a time, not long ago, when tattoos were considered the exclusive practice sailors and bikers. All this has changed as the members of Generation X have embraced tattoos and other forms of personal body modification. While tattoos are an ancient art, even having been found on the four thousand-year-old man recently discovered in the Alps, we are making it our own in new and creative ways.

A small, basic tattoo usually starts at fifty dollars and up, but top tattoo artists can charge a hundred or more dollars an hour for detailed work or larger pieces. Some of us choose to have meaningful slogans or symbols placed on our bodies, while others favor body art that can cover our backs, arms, chests, and other areas. Of course, it can be less expensive to have a friend tattoo you, but this doesn't guarantee the quality or safety of going to a trained, licensed tattooist.

There are even more extreme ways of decorating our bodies: branding and scarification. Branding involves burning a design into the skin, while scarification is a more complicated process that involves lifting the skin with a needle so that it scars over in the desired pattern. While these are less common, they have become popular among those of our generation who seek to go beyond the old taboos, and who may regard mere tattoos as too "safe." And brands and scars are a great deal more permanent than tattoos.

As famous film director John Waters *(Polyester, Serial Mom)* recently commented, "Someone's going to make a fortune taking the tattoos off this generation when they get older." This is already possible through the use of laser treatments that "erase" the ink under the skin, which gives us the luxury of changing our minds later in life—but older people like Waters may not give us enough credit when it comes to sticking with our decisions. Plenty of our tattoos are going to stay with us to the bitter end, true testaments of our dedication to freedom and personal expression.

Tweaked Out to Vampire Time

Tweaked Out

To be in a state of disarray; to be unresponsive and lethargic; to be defective.

Tweeker/Tweaker

1) White-trash crystal methamphetamine enthusiast, often a cart pusher, dumpster diver, turbohiker, speedy guy. This one does crystal as a lifestyle and is not to be trusted.

2) A crack addict with a skateboard.

Twentysomethings

Those in their twenties. Twentysomethings are delaying marriage, delaying plans, living at home with parents or other relatives for economic reasons, and are spending much of their money on pleasure.

Twitchers

Video games that require frequent pushing of buttons. Usually fighting, shooting, and chasing arcade-type games. Also called Thumb-twitchers.

Ubermensch

German term coined by Friedrich Nietzsche to describe his vision of a superior human being; can be translated as "superman." Now used ironically to put down someone who acts as if they're better than others, morally or otherwise: "Oh, you're such an Ubermensch!"

Unreal Estate

1) Cyberspace.

2) A place not of this reality. "The only type of unreal estate she can own has nothing to do with land."

URL

Uniform Resource Locator. Simply, an individual address on the World Wide Web.

Vamp Do

Slur aimed at a bad or odd hairstyle.

Vampire Time

A schedule where one sleeps all day and haunts clubs and coffeehouses at night. Refers to writers, artists, slackers, club kids, and other bohemian types (see **Phase Shifters**).

FILE   EDIT   DELETE   HELP   Self-Destruct X

TWENTYSOMETHINGS

The time when life's possibilities are wide open. Everybody seems happy to tell me I should be doing with my life, but really—isn't that for me to decide? There are so many options available that I'm not willing to lock myself into a single one for the rest of my life. Not yet, and maybe not ever.

I'm not being indecisive—I'm exploring my choices and developing my potential. Yeah, sure, there's nothing systematic about the way I'm doing it, but isn't that the point? If I make mistakes—and I'm sure I will—then I'll probably learn from them sooner or later. I've already seen people my age make the really big mistake of digging themselves into a job rut just for the sake of comfort and security. When they crash and burn from the pressure, it isn't a pretty sight. I'm not letting myself get caught up in that vicious circle. It's better to live on the edge, working without a net. It helps keep your eyes and mind open.

For some reason, some people may think this is selfish, but I don't agree. I'm not an idealist, but I believe there are important issues our generation needs to deal with. But if we jump in and try to fix things without first being aware of our own strengths and weaknesses, we might just make a bigger mess of things than the generations before us. That's why it's so important for people like me to take this time to grow and learn at a natural rate.

THIRTYSOMETHINGS

This is the time one starts feeling some biological pressures. Like, by now I'm supposed to be grown up and have it all figured out.

I miss my twenties some, but my thirties are starting out easier. I feel like I'm more in control, more responsible. Now I understand that nobody else knows what they are doing either, though some don't realize it, and this usually makes them pathetic or dangerous.

Vapid to Vid

Vapid
Lacking spirit.

Vapidly Beautiful
Beauty, but no brains.

Vaporware
Software, ideas, or slogans that don't perform when it comes down to actually using them or relying on them.

Vaselines, The
Scottish quartet led by Eugene Kelly and Frances McKee that only lasted a couple of years (1990–1992). During that time, they cut about twenty raw, quite melodic tunes. They broke up and that might have been the end, except that **Nirvana** recorded two of their tunes on "Incesticide" and their music was instantly in the revival bins. Sub Pop issued "The Way of the Vaselines: A Complete History" in 1992, and it is a must-have album among alternative pop fans. Kelly went on to form Captain America, which became Eugenius, a quite successful alternative pop band.

Veejay
An MTV video DJ (see **MTV**).

Vegan/Vegetarian
Person who does not eat meat. As the death of noted vegetarian River Phoenix has shown, the meatless lifestyle does not have to be a dull or safe one. Many recreational, and sometimes quite dangerous, drugs contain no meat and are not tested on animals!

Verite
A term that connotes that certain *je ne sais quois*, that *savoir faire* (see **Je Ne Sais Quois**). This actually describes something that is genuine but it is a word few X'ers would genuinely use. It may be another attempt to upgrade the lingo by using words with foreign appeal; "It's French, so it must be good." One X-critic said, "That's a *Spin* magazine word."

Vid
1) A video or videogames.

2) A nickname for Sid Vicious of the band The Sex Pistols, considered by many to be the original punk-rock band (see **Punk [Music]**).

FILE EDIT DELETE HELP Self-Destruct X

WHAT'S A VEGAN GONNA DO?

Boomer Mom to Gen X'er: "Eat your pot roast or you won't get any ice cream and cake." Now we know she was telling us to "eat this chemical-, fat-, and cholesterol-laden dead cow or you won't get any sugary, high-fat, yellow-dye-number 13–laden synthetic milk product."

The love of meat continues to prevent any real change. Burning the rain forests to make grazing land for animals raised and brutally slaughtered to provide the animal products with which we poison our bodies. The soil is soon depleted and abandoned to erosion. Then new bites are ripped from the flesh of Mother Earth.

Our bodies are diseased and fattened, our brains are sickened, yet we scream for more: "Give me four double beef Gluttonwoppers and a ham croissant." "That'll be $8.53 at the first window please. . . . Next. . . ."

Vid Clerk

Video-store clerk (as in Quentin Tarantino).

Videodrome

A 1982 film by director David Cronenberg, starring James Woods, in which TV broadcasting begins to take over reality as well as the hero's body. The recurring line "All hail the new flesh" later became a catchphrase for those who see the personal computer and the **Internet** as a means for humanity to escape its physical limitations in cyberspace.

Vig

As in Butch Vig, glossy knob twirler for such MTV superstars as Nirvana, Smashing Pumpkins, and others. Nirvana was so put off by the amazing success of their songs with Vig's production that they enlisted noisemeister Steve Albini, an indie stalwart, to produce their next, and last, studio album (see **Knob Twirler, Indie Band, MTV, Nirvana,** and **Noisemeister**).

Virtual Communities

Collections of like-minded people who meet on line and share ideas on everything from politics to punk rock. The global village is full of tiny electronic subdivisions made up of cold-fusion physicists, white supremacists, gerontologists, and Grateful Deadheads. Like any other community, each has its own in-jokes, cliques, bozos, and bores.

Virtual Reality

Artificial, computer-generated, 3-D environments in which special goggles, gloves, body suits, and other devices enable the user to move about and interact in an imaginary world.

Voice Jail

A voice-mail system so poorly designed that the caller feels trapped and hangs up.

Wack Slacks

Old, ripped jeans. The kind of jeans you can sell back to those hustling street fashion stores for $20. Although invented as part of the infamous *New York Times* Grunge Hoax (see **Grunge Hoax**), this phrase has found its way into actual use.

Wacked Out

To be crazy.

ADVERTISING/TARGET X

Lately, car manufacturers, booze companies, clothing manufacturers and marketers from all walks of life are desperate to sell, sell, sell to Generation X. Does it matter that the press still views us as lazy, MTV-watching kiddies going nowhere? Not at all. Because as far as Madison Avenue is concerned, X'ers have proven they like toys—and advertisers spend their money accordingly.

Brokerage firms spout statistics like crazy: "The rise in the number of twenty-five year olds has been a major catalyst to the economy. . . ." "The economic stimuli from twentysomethings is boosting the nation's gross national product. . . " Jeep Wranglers; cheap, hip furniture manufacturers IKEA; and clothing superstores Urban Outfitters all reported huge increases in sales in the last two years—almost all of it accounted for by the under-thirty set.

The problem is, those very folks on Madison Avenue are way too into pegging X'ers into one big focus group—Target X—which we hate.

We grew up on television, and we understand the myths and lies that TV propels as reality. Our healthy skepticism is a shield that advertisers find hard to get past. We might admit that we do have a jaded sense of self, though . . . especially when it comes to the onslaught of advertising.

Even so, sometimes we eat it up—provided it's humorous, technologically fascinating, and smug. Smug is good. The average Gen X'er actually likes advertising. We enjoy commercials. But usually, we're more into how things are marketed than we are into the product itself. If something looks too much like MTV, or features generic Gen X'ers in flannels and goatees, it's lame. It screams "someone old conceived

(continued on p. 181)

Wag
Moron.

Wall
To lean against the wall at a party. A fine example of Generation X's skill at condensing the terminology of the previous generation (wall-flower) into more compact packaging.

Wank (male)
To jerk off, pull the pud, beat it, make a date with Rosy and her five sisters, or otherwise masturbate.

Wank Ware
Digital pornography, pornographic software.

Wannabe
Trying to be or appear to be something you are not. It takes more than long hair, a scruffy beard, and a guitar to be the next **Nirvana.** Without talent, you're just another **Kurt Cobain** wannabe.

Wastoid
A person throwing their life away on drugs or booze in order to stay permanently wasted.

Waxing the Dolphin
Surfer lingo for wanking (see **Wank**).

Way
Sure, yes, of course; as an answer to "no way." (From *Wayne's World*.)

Weasel
One who constantly scams their friends out of money, rides, or a place to crash. A professional sponge, or an acquaintance possessing sponge-like qualities. A more dangerous variety of weasel wears suits for camouflage and frequently inhabits the music or movie industry.

Web
Short for World Wide Web (see **World Wide Web**).

Web Browser
Any program used to access the World Wide Web, e.g., Netscape Navigator and NCSA Mosaic.

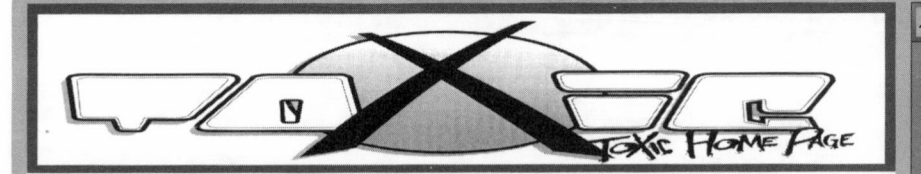

ADVERTISING/TARGET X
(continued from p. 179)

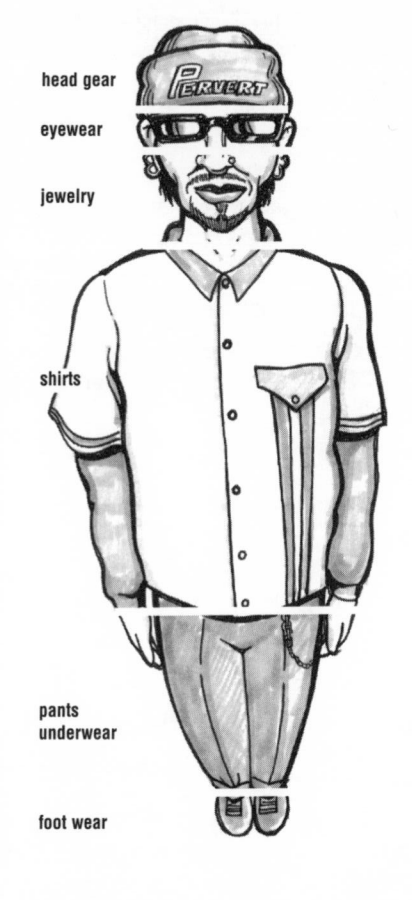

head gear

eyewear

jewelry

shirts

pants
underwear

foot wear

this as hip and youthful and Gen X-ish."And there's nothing worse than ad campaigns that get played to death. They don't take root in our unconscious—they just become annoying. Selling big and selling loud doesn't play, either. We might laugh at it, but we sure as hell aren't going to buy it.

MERCHING X

The Greater Talent Network, which normally makes its money booking celebrities on the lecture circuit, is putting together day-long seminars called X-Fests. These will feature youthful savants who both belong to and have pontificated about the generation. Among the speakers: Richard Linklater, who directed the Generation X movie *Slacker,* and Mark Leyner, author of *My Cousin, My Gastroenterologist.* For anywhere between $20,000 and $100,000—depending on how many of them a marketer wants to listen to—these downy-cheeked gurus will detail what makes them and their peer tick. (*Forbes* magazine)

Weenie

1) Substandard; uncool, geekish.

2) A wimpy person; dork.

Weltanschauung

Any specific world view. The world view that has dominated Western society since the eighteenth century has been the idea of progress—moral and material—through reason, science, democracy, and capitalism. The postmodern world view is against "grand narratives," is oriented toward diversity, and is more carnivalesque—a carnival of many voices, the spirit of **Generation X.**

Whif

1) To fall.

2) To hurt oneself. "He got whiffed on that one."

Wig On

1) To carry on, to keep doing what one is doing.

2) To physically move, travel, i.e., to come to one's domicile (hopefully bearing gifts from the local 7-11). "Hey, why don't you wig on over with a 12-pack."

Wig Out

To lose control of one's emotions. "When he saw his girlfriend ride off with that biker, he totally wigged out."

Wigger

White gangster.

Wigger Hat

A colorful, oversized stocking cap that hangs loose to one side.

Wilding

Traveling the streets by car or foot, searching out and randomly shooting complete strangers. Originally this word may have been a hoax, but now it accurately describes the activities of a few misguided, sick souls. "One of those words that some reporter heard somewhere, and in a fit of paranoid journalism, it gave all you Baby Boomers one more thing to lose your burrito over." Though invented as part of the infamous *New York Times* Grunge Hoax, this phrase has found its way into actual use (see **Grunge Hoax**).

Wilding

"Honk if you've never seen an Uzi shot out of a back window."

Wilma

Female moron. (Mrs. Flintstone.)

Woodshedding

A musician's term describing long, hard hours of practicing with no distractions or interruptions. A similar phrase is "deep in the shed." It's amusing lingo like this that musicians use to further separate themselves from those who merely listen to music.

WOOFs

Well-Off Older Folks.

Woopie

Well-Off Older Person.

Wunderkind

Originally a prodigy, a wonder child. Now it is used to describe someone of great potential, of whom much is expected.

Wuss/Wussies

Wimp, a pusillanimous person lacking courage or resolution who is marked by disgusting timidity. Also used as a verb. "He wussed out on us and never showed up to help."

X-iled

1) Lost in the wilderness of the modern era and twentysomething.

2) The title of a book of collected stories edited by Michael Wexler and John Hulme.

X-ing

Tripping on the drug Ecstasy or X (see **Ecstasy/Extasy**).

Y Generation

The generation born during the years 1982–2004. The Millennium Generation.

Yack

To vomit.

Yahoo!

With the mind-boggling glut of information on the Internet, it's hard to know where to turn. Yahoo is one of the leading **Internet** directories available, and the one with the coolest name. Simply by typing

(continued)

FILE   EDIT   DELETE   HELP   Self-Destruct X

SOCIAL (IN)SECURITY

If there's one thing Generation X has the right to complain about, it's the fact that our future security is being used up now by Silents and Boomers. We're paying into Medicare and Social Security now, but by the time *we* need them, there won't be much to pass around—unless we dedicate ourselves to doing something to change the way things work. As things stand, even the Social Security Administration says it may be broke by the year 2020, and definitely by 2029. Face it—we need to radically change the way the federal government handles these entitlement programs. And while we're at it, we're going to have to change its priorities, and its leaders, by replacing them with our own.

Social Security is the main problem. We can't count on it being there for us when we start to turn gray. The reason is simple. As it stands, Social Security is not the trust it's sup-

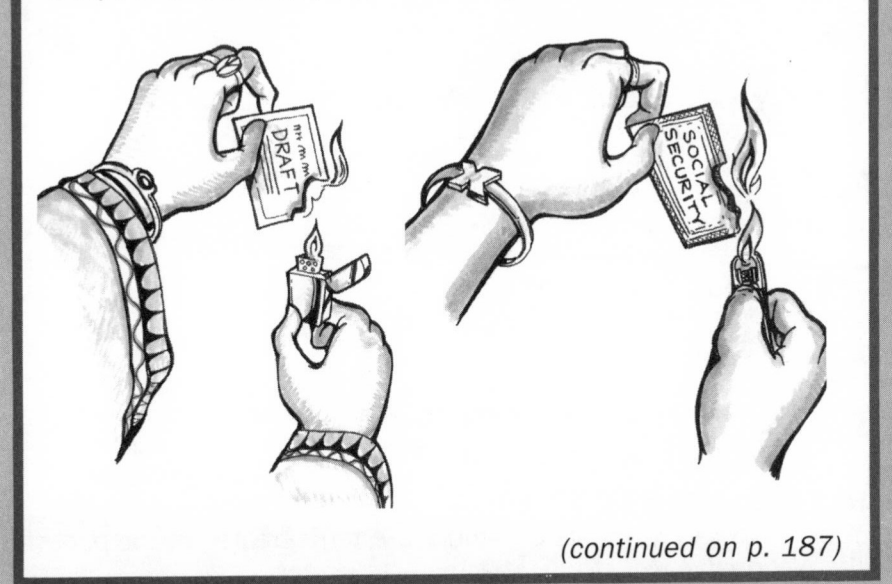

(continued on p. 187)

in a key word or two, users can generate a list of related sites on the World Wide Web. Similar services are provided by Infoseek (a larger service) and other companies (see **Internet** and **World Wide Web**).

YAPs
Young Aspiring Professionals.

YAVIS
Those who are Young, Attractive, Verbal, Intelligent, and Successful.

Yeepies
Youthful, Energetic, Elderly People Involved in Everything.

Yippie
1) Young Indictable Professional Person, a name born of the insider stock-trading scandals of the '80s. Not to be confused with:

2) Member of the Youth International Party, which became known in the late '60s for civil disobedience and antiwar protests.

Yo
"Hi, what's up?"

Yo, Bro
"Hello, friend!"

Yo, G
Hello, gangsta!

Yo Homey G-Skillet Homeperson
Saying hi to a friend while making fun of him/her.

Yorkie
A New York yuppie (see **Yuppie**).

YUCA
Young, Upwardly-mobile Cuban American.

Yuffie
Young Urban Failure, generally a Baby Boomer making less than $15,000 a year.

Yuckie
Young, Upwardly-mobile Communist. A term created in the pages of the *National Review* for Gorbachev's supporters.

SOCIAL (IN)SECURITY *(continued from p. 185)*

posed to be. It's just another Boomer and Silent Generation rip-off of future generations, starting with ours but affecting all generations down the line.

Even though we can't afford it, we pay a much larger portion of our paychecks toward Social Security than Boomers or Silents, but they are the ones who are getting to use the hard-earned cash we're giving up now. It's pretty discouraging for a Gen X'er who earns $9 an hour (less than $20,000 a year, before deductions) to realize that he or she is helping fund the Social Security and Medicare of a retired couple who earn $50,000 a year and own a house with no mortgage. Seniors are the most affluent segment of our population, but the U.S. government spends eleven times more, per capita, on them than it does on children, the poorest part of the population.

Of course, the Boomers and Silent Generations' reaction to all this is predictable. It's all too easy for them to dismiss our concerns as juvenile whining—but nothing could be farther from the truth. These are valid concerns, and we're just expressing a healthy, justified skepticism and an unwillingness to be enslaved economically, and robbed of our future. The people who started this country did so with one eye on the prosperity of future generations, but it seems some generations have forgotten this. It's up to us not only to remember this, but to put these ideals back into action so our grandchildren won't have reason to resent us.

Luckily, the days of the Boomer and Silent Generations' political domination of the United States are coming to an end. As we move into our newfound political responsibilities, we will set our nation's priorities and control the operation of our government. Every generation has the right—and the obligation—to decide its own future. We mean to see to it that the generations that follow us won't have to fight for these rights, but will be able to enjoy them freely *(see p. 191)*.

Yummie

Young, Upwardly-Mobile Mommy.

Yumpie

Young, Upwardly-Mobile Professional.

Yuppiegate

Scandals based on Yuppie greed.

Yuppie

Young Urban Professional with a taste for BMWs, Rolex watches, jogging suits, imported bottled water, and fashionable restaurants; often self-centered with much-larger-than-is-good-for-anyone egos.

Yuppietax

A tax that primarily hits Yuppies, like a tax on health-club memberships.

Zap TV Viewers

Those who turn television channels too quickly, too often.

Zeitgeist

A German word made up of *zeit* ("time") and *geist* ("spirit"). Literally, the spirit of the time, the intellectual and moral trend of an age or period (see **Global Zeitgeist**).

Zine

Small press magazine, often hand made *sans* computers. Independently owned magazines that attempt to move beyond the strata of Corporate Amerika.

Zippies

1) A cultural phenomenon marked by an unlikely fusion of dance-scene hedonism, cyber street tech, and pagan spirituality. Started in Great Britain, the movement had little luck connecting with its counterparts in the USA, but the term has been applied over here as well.

2) Sometimes used as a put down based on the title character of the cartoon strip "Zippy the Pinhead." A sarcastic and weird look at life and people, this strip is carried in many small and/or **alternative** publications.

3) Condoms.

ZIPPY THE PINHEAD

A Zippies cartoon series by Bill Griffith, syndicated nationally.

"The last things I like about Zippy are the way semantic pies splatter on the walls of reason, philosophical spring sausages lead out of improbable containers, and rubber hatchets chop at the very foundations of our existence. Am I finished yet?"

B. Kliban, from the Introduction of *Zippy Stories,* a collection of Zippy cartoons published by Last Gasp, Inc., of San Francisco.

Zon
The horizon.

Zooed Out
To be overcrowded.

Zup
A greeting used to ask how one's day is going. A handy contraction of "What's up?"

Zup America?

THE TOXIC TIMES

Saturday, January 1, 2000

Generations X and Y Launch Hostile Takeover of U.S.

Today, newly elected X'er President Hillary Love announced bold plans to decisively win the Great Generational Civil War here in the United States.

At her first press conference held in the White House Rose Garden, the successful Third Millennium Party candidate followed through on her campaign promise to defeat the remaining Second Millennium Forces.

"I have directed the Attorney General to place the United States federal government into bankruptcy. This will wipe out all of the debt and entitlement obligations the Silent and Boomer generations tried to stick us with. Social Security and Medicare are really their problems anyway.

"Next we will execute a leveraged buyout from the federal government to take the entire West Coast. The Japanese Twenty-first-Century Party has already agreed to provide the financing. Hawaii will be sold to them, Alaska to Texaco and Washington and Oregon to Weyerhauser Lumber Company.

"Then we will remove the seniors from California and franchise the entire state to Club Med.

"Following that, we will go after the East Coast and do the same thing with Florida and some other states."

"The Silents and Boomers can't complain about hostile takeovers, leveraged buyouts, and vulture asset stripping. They are the ones who perfected the techniques."

As news of President Love's announcement spread, newly elected young leaders from other nations around the world announced intentions to develop similar plans.

Leaders of the demoralized Democratic and Republican parties could not be reached for comment. They are reported to still be in hiding from the angry constituent mobs that only last week destroyed each party's national headquarters.

PIERCING

Faced with the ever-growing threat of mainstream mediocrity, some of us are taking control of our own bodies and express our personal freedom with ornaments. Piercing, tattoos, brands, and scarification marks us as unique individuals and shows our defiance of a society that wants everyone to look and think the same. Extreme body ornamentation announces our knowledge that we are in control of our own society and our own generation.

Body piercing used to be a primarily gay phenomenon, but in the past decade, more people, both gay and heterosexual, have taken to it, using it to separate themselves from the pillars of normalcy. Punk rockers of the early eighties were the originators of this trend, and now piercing has spread throughout Generation X—just another signal that announces, loud and clear, that we are not like the Boomers and Silents. Face it—we're a hell of a lot more daring!

While some people still get their piercings done by a friend with a pin and some rubbing alcohol, most choose to go to a professional piercer, where precision and hygiene are guaranteed. (A professional piercer is one who has studied under an experienced piercer with an intense knowledge of various techniques and methods.) While piercing guns were in vogue a while

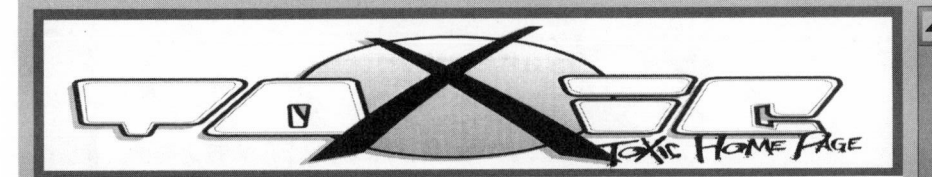
back, needles are now more common. Needles allow for large gauge openings and more permanent piercings.

Piercing comes in many varieties. The most obvious include nose piercings (of both nostrils and septum) and navel piercings. Tongue, nipple, and genital piercings are much less obvious, and are often adopted for sensual reasons rather than for open display. Eyebrow, lip, and cheek piercings are much less common because these areas move more, which can cause scarring, infections, and other healing problems. Jewelry for piercings is also varied. Rings, barbells, and studs can be made from gold, silver, steel and other metals.

Jewelry prices can range from inexpensive (around $5) to hundreds of dollars or more, depending on the quality of the metal used. A first piercing will generally cost $25 to $40, but additional piercings can cost half that, or less. With the proliferation of shops that specialize in piercing, body modification has become accessible to most of Generation X during the past three years. For just $60 and an afternoon away from work, you can take the first step away from conformity and join the radical fashion fringe of our generation.

ENVIRONMENT

It's no wonder that, with all this talk about Gen X's distrust of their elders and the world they have created, their dissatisfaction would find a home in the biggest picture of all: the Earth and the desire to "save it" from the hands of those who have come before. That quest for finding the best way to salvage, that search for the perfect environmentalism, has turned up thousands of factions of youthful globers hell-bent on waving the flag of aid.

Typical Gen-X philosophy: While the earth may be able to recover from the acts of nature, which wreak havoc on global ecosystems, it will definitely have trouble recovering from the additional human havoc.

But most Gen-X'ers aren't extremists screaming that the end of the world is happening tomorrow. No: They say, "Okay, we've poked a few holes in the sky, thrown several volcanoes worth of junk into it, plus some stuff that no volcano ever spewed, and chopped down and burned most of the huge forests that cleaned the crap out of the air. But the planet will survive all this— it just won't be a very nice place to live. Ever see *Logan's Run*?

"And by the way, the replanted forests are not the indigenous breeds. They just graze cows over land that

may have grown a plant that could have cured cancer. Oh, and how does that steak taste? Do you know you could have fed a great many people on the grain that fed that cow you're devouring?"

From global warming issues to veganism, X'ers are trying to align their personal choices with global concerns. It's a pretty noble effort—provided we really are concerned. That pretty peace sign on the back of your beat-up truck, that groovy tie-dye with the Grateful Dead message on the back—are they sincere statements, or just empy slogans? There are all kinds of environmentalists in the mix—true believers and posers. For the posers, environmentalism is just this year's fad.

Even so, you'll find more twentysomethings truly asking the question: "How can we save the environment and have a good time doing it?" And many are really striving to come up with real solutions: rethinking the personal as political—as consumer, worker, employer, saver/investor, voter, policy shaper or rate payer—and live life with purpose, excitement, and satisfaction.

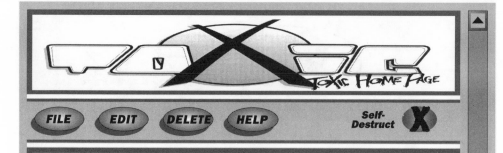

EMPLOYMENT/ECONOMIC EXPECTATIONS

Good employment opportunities for us should become a national priority. The Boomers and Silents in Washington can't continue to pursue their own agendas, ignoring us, and our needs and rights as citizens.

Today the job market for us is extremely tough and disheartening and it is going to worsen. Corporate downsizing, global competition and just plain greed continue to eliminate many (sometimes it seems like almost all) jobs that offer reasonable pay, benefits, and a chance for career advancement. (See **McJob**).

The largest employer in the United States is not General Motors, but Manpower, Inc., the temporary employment agency. Service-sector, low-paying, basically temporary without adequate benefits jobs are rapidly overwhelming the job market we face.

Solutions can be found and implemented for this problem. It's not one unique to us today. Almost all nations face it periodically and deal with it. However, our government does little to correct this. Many times it actually makes life worse by doing things like cutting back student-loan programs, or making it financially impossible for companies to set up training programs.

We are growing in political strength and will soon decide who goes to Washington. The politicians who listen to us will stay, the ones that don't, won't.

"The only way I'll ever own a home is if I'm lucky enough to inherit one."

THE MORE THINGS CHANGE

"The shows were broader, the buildings were higher, the morals were loose, and the liquor was cheaper; but all these did not really minister much delight. Young people wore out early—they were hard and languid at twenty-one. . . . The city was bloated, glutted, stupid with cakes and circuses, and a new expression, 'O Yeah?' summed up all the enthusiasm evoked by the announcement of the last super-skyscrapers."

(F. Scott Fitzgerald, 1896–1940)

ACKNOWLEDGMENTS

We would like to thank the creators of the following sources of information on popular culture. Their work provided invaluable aid in the preparation of this book.

Generation Ecch! by Jason Cohen and Michael Krugman (Fireside Books,1994)
Generation X: Tales For An Accelerated Culture by Douglas Coupland (St. Martin's Press, 1991)
Life After God by Douglas Coupland (Pocket Books, 1994)
Alt.Culture: An A–Z of the 90s— Underground, Online and Over-the- Counter by Steven Daly and Nathaniel Wice (Harper Collins, 1995)
Official Slacker Handbook by Sarah Dunn (Warner Books, 1994)
Generations: The History of America's Future, 1584 to 2069 by Neil Howe and William Strauss (Quill/William Morrow, 1991)
13th Gen: Abort, Retry, Ignore, Fail? by Neil Howe and William Strauss (Vintage Books, 1993)
Covert Culture Sourcebook 1.0 by Richard Kadrey (St. Martin's Press, 1993)
Covert Culture Sourcebook 2.0 by Richard Kadrey (St. Martin's Press, 1994)
Revolution X: A Survival Guide for Our Generation by Rob Nelson and Jon Cowan (Penguin Books, 1994)
Marketing To Generation X by Karen Ritchie (Lexington Books, 1995)
Mondo 2000: A User's Guide To The New Edge, edited by Rudy Rucker, R.U. Sirius and Queen Mu (HarperCollins, 1992)
Cyberia by Douglas Rushkoff (HarperCollins, 1994)
The Gen X Reader by Douglas Rushkoff (Ballantine Books, 1994)
Voices of the Xiled, edited by Michael Wexler and John Hulme (Doubleday, 1994)
Billy Idol by Mike Wrenn (Omnibus Press, 1991)

Advertising Age
Axcess
Billboard
Brandweek
Business Week
Columbia Journal Review Details
The Economist
Editor and Publisher
Entertainment Weekly
Forbes Magazine
Hypno
Mondo 2000
Multimedia World
The New Republic
Newsweek
Rolling Stone
Slamm
Soma
Spin
Thrasher
Urb
U.S. News and World Report
Utne Reader
Vogue
Wired Magazine
The Chicago Tribune
The Los Angeles Times
The New York Times
The San Diego Union
The Seattle Times
USA Today
The Washington Post
CompuServe
Wayne's World (Paramount, 1992. Directed by Penelope Spheeris)
New Jack City (Warner Bros., 1991. Directed by Mario Van Peebles)
Clueless (Paramount, 1995. Directed by Amy Heckerling)
MTV

We also thank the many people who were interrogated, interviewed (often without their knowledge), beseeched, and begged, who we have shamefully neglected to recognize.

And a final note of thanks to Seaside Publishing Services for bringing the appearance of order to chaos.